THE PROSPECTOR

GO FOR THE GOLD

GO FOR THE GOLD!

(Or How to Pay For Your Vacation)

William G. Hainsworth
P.Eng.

Price Publishing,
Blaine ,WA.

First Printing 1991

Library of Congress Cataloguing in Publication Data 91-67978

Hainsworth, William George
Go For The Gold!

Bibliography: p.
1. Gold Placering and Panning — Locations, equipment etc.

ISBN 1-880868-00-8

Printed in the United States of America

Dedication

To my wife, Elizabeth, and my family, Bob and Melody, George and Liz-Ann,without whose loving help this book might have been more difficult.

Acknowledgements

The writer gratefully acknowledges the following organizations, or individuals, who courteously supplied photographs for insertion into this book.

Arizona Historical Society Library.
California State Library.
Nevada Historical Society.
Vancouver Public Library.
Wells Fargo Bank of San Francisco.
R.M. Bottom of Tonopah.
Cassandra Resources Inc.
Mintun Mining Group.

Cover Design: A. Abercrombie

CONCERNING THE AUTHOR

William G. Hainsworth, P.Eng., is a Canadian geologist raised in Southern Ontario who received his Bachelor of Science Degree in Honours Geology from the University of Western Ontario in London, Ontario in 1950. Previously he had spent some four war years in Great Britain attached to the Royal Canadian Air Force as a Radar Engineer.

Upon graduation, Mr. Hainsworth started developing his background experience by working at the underground gold mines in Northern Ontario and Quebec. From here he ventured into field exploration which saw him travelling into all the states of the Union and the provinces of Canada. He became well-known for his expertise on gold, both from the lode and placer viewpoints. As a consultant, he visited many gold developments offering his suggestions on improvements of operations.

Over his forty years of mining background he has been successful in bringing into production some three major mines in North America. His advice has added to the operational life of many placer and lode operations.

Mr. Hainsworth had the designation "Professional Engineer" bestowed upon him in 1964 when he successfully brought a molybdenum mine into operation in a financially depressed area. His subsequent success with two major mining operations added lustre to his name.

Mr. Hainsworth is in a semi-retirement stage at the present time but the attraction, and his devotion to mining, has been instrumental in his writing this book.

INTRODUCTION

It was while contemplating moving into a semi-retirement mode that the idea of this book was presented to me. My wife, probably sensing the uncertainties I was feeling about the future and also to ensure that I would not be underfoot to interfere with the normal progress of housekeeping, suggested I write a book. A book that would condense all forty-two years of mining experience into a volume that would be entertaining, and probably educational, to others.

I had always enjoyed my field work whether involved with hardrock (lode) or placer. My experience had taken me everywhere on the North American continent.

However I could see a need for a less technical, more down to earth approach to the subject of placer mining for the layman. In particular I could see the weekend prospector or the recreational vehicle owner on holidays wondering what to do and where to go. So I sought to describe the wonderful world of placer deposits in language understood by all. My wife edited my writings with the admonishment that if she understood then certainly others would. This was a warning to me to lay off the technical terminology and the stilted embodiments of my professional reports. So I have labored!

I realized that not everybody was prepared to hike into the unknown, setup a tent, battle bears or snakes, and thoroughly enjoy oneself while panning. In this modern age of recreation we like to combine the outdoors with a little of the indoors. So into being came the "nearest campground" and/or "motel" as a designation in the placer locations.

The first eight chapters deal with the birth of a placer deposit and how to attack it. I've thrown in chapters on field supplies (and tried to relate present costs to them), expanding into a small family dynasty, and have even gone historical by dredging up ancient gold reminiscences. In addition I've shown how to stake your own claim and how to protect it. I've supplied charts and figures for easy conversions. Why I've even passed on addresses of purchasers of your gold!

The last three chapters deal primarily with known placer operations at various locations in the southwestern states—Arizona, California and Nevada.

As you will notice there are numerous instances of placer workings scattered throughout these three states. Many go back beyond 1850 while others became prominent during the desperation years — the Great Depression of 1930-1938.

The average prospector knows what he is looking for and generally finds it. Few new placer finds are coming to light today. The old ones are being reworked and reworked.

The original placer finds were located by inquisitive prospectors in the early decades of the 1800's. They knew the signs and what to look for. Prior to them the Mexican miners had moved into certain areas of Arizona and Lower California. Their hunt had been initiated by the Spanish Conquistadors' and the subsequent journeys of the various Franciscan and Jesuit monks. The Spanish Empires' greed for gold is well documented.

The early surface deposits in the creeks and the dry gulches were quickly located and just as quickly exhausted. The prospectors moved on looking for more of the easily located "Recent" placer deposits. As these became less obvious and thus more difficult to find, they suddenly realized the presence of the ancient "Tertiary" stream beds. So the switch to the high level terraces and the deeply buried old river courses. Shafts were sunk and drifts run out — the Tertiary beds were worked.

The Chinese placer miners followed the prospectors. Once a stream, or a gulch, was abandoned, the Chinese moved in and reworked the old tailings. The very thoroughness of their procedure left little behind. Whereas the initial finder took all the high-grade ore, the Chinese cleaned out the low-grade.

The Chinese worked the surface showings; they seldom ventured into the underground workings.

The process of erosion continues; it never ceases. Gravel, sand, clay and gold are still being deposited. But as the original placer findings were the buildup of eons, today's depositions are slow and small in the time frame.

There are probably placer streams and gulches that have never been discovered. Wherever water rolls down a sidehill or wind blows through a gulch, the possibility of a hidden gold-quartz vein being exposed with subsequent erosion and deposition exists.

The placer locations given in the last three chapters have not been visited by the writer. However I have visited quite a few on which professional operations were, or are, proceeding. I was not one of those happy souls who chased down the gold presence, placered it and returned to an everyday existence or ventured on to find another stream or wash. My presence in the field was professional — to examine and make recommendations to those larger placer organizations already engaged in, or contemplating, operations. This does not mean that I did not do my fair share of initial field examinations accompanied by panning. It only means that I envied those who could devote all their time to the search, location and production of gold. So I say to you — if you have the time, the means and the yearning then GO FOR THE GOLD!

CONTENTS

Chapter 1

THE LURE OF GOLD

Of all the elements on this earth, gold has been the most sought. Since earliest times the cry of "gold" has taken men across oceans, continents, over towering mountain peaks, through the jungles, into the arctic wastelands, and across scorching deserts. Expeditions were sent, men died, countries were conquered, all because of the lure of this elusive metal.

The Myths

Over the centuries, alchemists have striven to turn baser metals into that most noble of elements: gold. In mythology, we are told of Jason's search and struggle to locate the Golden Fleece. And of King Midas' greed for the metal, which led to his only daughter being turned into a gold statue. In history, the acquisition of gold, and its resulting power led to Cortes' and Pizarro's conquest of Mexico and Peru.

The original discovery of gold has been lost in antiquity. References date back to the ancient writings of the Chinese, Hindus, and Hebrews, and it is mentioned early in the Old Testament. Centuries ago, the Egyptians mined and processed gold, as evidenced by the tombs of the Pharaohs. In an

Egyptian ruling thought to be about 3500 B.C., the economics of the precious metals was defined as 2 $^1/_2$ parts of silver to be the equivalent to one part of gold in value.

The Old Testament refers frequently to two legendary sources of gold: Ophir and Havilah. Theologians and scientists still ponder the location of these sites. Ophir is defined as that country from which the navies of King Solomon brought precious metals and jewels back to his kingdom and is thought to contain the "Lost Mines of Solomon". Location of these mines has been variously sited in such localities as the Turkish Pontic gold area immediately south of the Black Sea; the reef extensions into what is now known as Zimbabwe; the gold mines of the Balkan Mountains in southern Turkey; the Sudan, and possibly, the ancient mines of Ethopia.

The term Havilah has also been thought to be the ancient name for the present Pontic gold fields of Turkey.

History tells us that in 2000 B.C. the Egyptians were mining gold and copper in the Sinai, eastern Egypt, and the Sudan (then known as Nubia, nub meaning gold). In 1600 B.C. Queen Hatshepsut was importing gold bullion from Zimbabwe. In 1300 B.C. as Egypt was developing its empire, it was also developing to a high degree the expertise required in mining and milling the various metals. They left behind a legacy of mining knowledge, which aided and abetted the

Persians, the Greeks, and finally, the Romans in their great empire expansions.

The Present

In the New World, the Indians of the Americas were aware of gold but did not place the same value on it as did the Old World. Columbus on one of his early expeditions, encountered gold nuggets displayed or worn by the natives. The news of this encounter so excited the Spaniards that expeditions were sent searching for the gold. These expeditions culminated in the conquest of the Mexican Aztecs and the South American Incas by the Spanish conquistadores.

Mining appears to have had some influence on colonization in later years. One of the early postulates concerning the origin of gold deposits concluded they were formed under the influence of the sun. Thus the settlement and exploration in the New World was initially confined to those areas near the equator. Later repudiation of this theory led to the extension of prospecting and colonization out of these constraints and into more temperate climates.

As mining effected colonization, so the converse is true. Mining did not go far afield from the colonies. Exploration for gold in Mexico, Chile and Peru attest to this. In the United States, gold prospecting pushed into Arizona, New Mexico and California.

The Great Rushes

It was in the latter state where on January 24, 1848 gold nuggets were found at Sutter's Mill on the American River. From these findings emanated the Great California Gold Rush of 1849-50. From there the prospecting spread into the hills of the Sierra Nevadas and in the following decade came the discoveries of the world-renowned Mother Lode, Grass Valley and Placerville in California, and the famous Comstock Lode in Nevada. In turn the Cripple Creek discovery in

Colorado (1891) was followed by the Nevada deposits at Tonopah and Goldfields in 1905.

It is of interest to note that placer deposits were sought first, and when these were exhausted, the resourceful prospectors and miners turned their attention to lode gold deposits. Incidentally the Australian Gold Rush of 1851 was started by an Australian prospector who had participated in the Californian rush. His discovery of high-grade, but short-lived, placer deposits near Bathhurst, New South Wales, paved the way for the famous lode discoveries of Kalgoorlie in Western Australia and the placer and lode deposits of Victoria and Queensland.

In 1870 the great Alaskan Gold Rush began. Centered in the Fairbanks region, it attracted hundreds of adventurers, some of whom had been in the California rush. This rush produced spectacular gold placer results, but like all placer rushes, it was exhausted in a few short years. However the extent and grade of the Alaskan placer deposits were instrumental in extending the life of many of these finds. Dredges have been an integral operational part of many of the placers in Alaska.

Discoveries in 1855 of gold in the Fraser River in British Columbia and in the Cariboo in 1859 lured many California miners to B.C. The richest placer discoveries and one of the last great gold rushes occurred in 1896 when the extremely high-grade gravels of a Yukon river inaugurated the Klondike Gold Rush. The town of Dawson, centered in this area, grew in 1896 from a population of 80 to a tent city of over 500 miners almost overnight.

With the advent of each new find, areas boom into existence. The migrating miners introduce new laws, establish new businesses and in doing so, open new frontiers. The ore runs out, or a "greater, much richer" find is announced in another locality. The migration begins again. The "boom" becomes a "bust" and often leaves behind a ghost town. No other industry opens frontiers so wide, so fast. Then having introduced "civilization" to the new world, moves on in a constant search for that most precious of all metals — gold!

Chapter 2

THE MANY FACES OF GOLD

Gold has fascinated man since prehistoric time. Its lustre and deep yellow color have created a feeling of warmth and security. In addition gold mining is a depression-proof industry, with a commodity that has no sales problem, and which generally is unaffected by overproduction or competition.

How do we identify gold? In what forms does gold appear? What are the minerals that bear close resemblance? How do we, as casual prospectors, collect the metal? Questions like these are important. We must be well acquainted with the answers before we hit the gold trail. If you are going to RV back into the mountains of Nevada or California, or walk up some dry wash in Arizona, then you will want to know what you are looking for, where you should expect to find it and, once identified, how to collect it! Let's first of all find out about this metal, gold.

Associates

Gold is a relatively common mineral. It is normally associated in nature with silver and, on occasions, copper. It has certain chemical and physical properties that distinguish it from other metals. To the layman, gold is often indistinguishable from pyrite, the latter known as "fool's gold". Gold is also similar in appearance to chalcopyrite, a copper mineral. Now let's find the differences.

Gold is a *native* mineral, that is, it is composed of only one element, gold. Pyrite is a mineral composed of two elements, sulphur and iron, while chalcopyrite has three elements, copper, sulphur and iron. Gold has the unique color of gold, a golden yellow, although if silver is an impurity within it, the color becomes much lighter. Pyrite, "fool's gold", on the other hand, has a pale yellow color while chalcopyrite is of a brass yellow, often tarnished lustre. All three are opaque minerals.

Hardness

Now we can also distinguish these three metals, and others, by the hardness test. The term hardness means the resistance that a smooth surface of a mineral offers to scratching, generally by a knife or a file. In the mineralogist's world there is a Scale of Hardness starting at one and working up to 10. This scale allows for a comparison of all known minerals. For example number one (which is exceedingly soft) is talc, while diamond (exceedingly hard) is number 10. Only another diamond will scratch a diamond. Number seven in the scale, for example, is quartz while number three in the scale is calcite. This scale is given in the appendix at the end. A knife is considered a 5 and therefore it will scratch all minerals in the groupings from 1 to 5, while not scratching those above. In the hardness scale gold is 2 1/2 to 3, easily scratched, pyrite is 6 to 6 1/2, difficult to scratch, and chalcopyrite is 3 1/2 to 4. Because it can be scratched so readily this is one area where gold can be distinguished from pyrite.

Figure 2-1: Early Miners

Crystal Shape

In physical shapes there are differences. Gold as a rule does not form good crystal structures. The crystals are irregularly distorted passing into very fine threads with intersecting and branching appearances or as irregular plates or scales. Seldom does gold appear as observable accumulations. In contrast pyrite and chalcopyrite often form large aggregates of crystalline appearance. Many times pyrite appears as numerous, scattered crystals in either a cubic form (six sided), or in its most frequent shape (from which the name was derived) pyritohedron (12 sided). Chalcopyrite, where crystallized, forms tetrahedrons (14 sided) but more often appears as solid masses of no particular shape. The sulphides, chalcopyrite and pyrite, (so named because they have sulphur associated with them) appear more frequently in crystal or massive form than gold.

Figure 2-2: Many Faces of Mining

Specific Gravity

However, the most important physical difference for amateur prospectors and gold panners is in the specific gravity of the minerals. The specific gravity of a mineral is a number which expresses the ratio between the mineral's weight and the weight of an *equal volume* of water (with water always being expressed as one). Pure gold has a specific gravity of 19.32 meaning one pound of pure gold will weight 19.32 times as heavy as an *equal volume* of water. By contrast chalcopyrite has a specific gravity of only 4.2 while pyrite has a specific gravity of 5.0. An equal volume of gold is almost 4 times as heavy as pyrite!! This heaviness is a very important factor in gold panning or placer mining. Some of the more common mineral specific gravities are listed in the appendix.

Other Features

Two other attributes of gold are its malleability and ductility. When gold is hammered out or drawn by heat it does so without cracking or breaking. In contrast pyrite and chalcopyrite are brittle and break easily when hammered . If you are still uncertain of that bright yellow metal, hit it with a hammer. If it shatters it is definitely not gold!! To elaborate further on these two physical properties, an ounce of gold can be beaten into foil some three hundred square feet in area or it can be drawn out into a wire over 40 miles in length!

An additional feature of gold is its solubility. Gold can not be dissolved in either nitric, hydrochloric or sulphuric acid. However it is soluble in aqua regia (the king of waters) which is a mixture of one part nitric acid mixed with two parts hydrochloric acid. Chalcopyrite is soluble in nitric acid as is pyrite.

Now another point of interest with gold is its reluctance to amalgamate or associate with other metals. When it does form another mineral the percentage of gold in the newly combined mineral is, as a rule, small. Some combinations which you are liable to run across either in nature or the written text are:

Arsenopyrite — arsenic, sulphur plus gold.
Stibnite — antimony, sulphur plus gold.
Sphalerite — zinc, sulphur plus gold and/or silver.
Galena — lead, sulphur plus silver and/or gold.
Calaverite — Tellurium plus gold.

There are others but these are the most common.

Silver and gold along with platinum form the precious metals group. Their purchase price is quoted in dollars "per ounce". The other metals are quoted "as dollars/cents per pound".

Where gold is associated with a mineral, or a mineral deposit, the adjective "auriferous" is used to designate the presence of the precious metal. Pyrite is frequently associated with gold deposits where the pyrite crystals often containing very minute amounts of gold. This type of pyrite is then termed auriferous pyrite and is noticeable only in lode deposits, that is the solid rock mineral deposits. Auriferous pyrite is not present in placer deposits.

Distribution

As a curiosity the proportion of gold (and its close associate silver) in the earth's crust is estimated to be roughly 0.005 parts per million for gold and and 0.05 parts per million for silver. This makes for a gold to silver ratio (in nature) of 0.1, or 1 part gold to every 10 parts silver.

The areal extent of the precious metals occurs widely distributed although in small amounts. Logically if they were in great quantity they wouldn't be "precious metals"! The chief source of gold is in the hypothermal gold-quartz veins. Hypothermal means being formed at high temperatures. In these veins, gold was deposited along with pyrite and other sulphides from deep, ascending mineral-bearing solutions winding up through cracks or fractures in the rocks. Normally in this type of vein deposit , the gold is so finely divided and uniformly distributed that its presence in the ore cannot be detected by the naked eye and requires a hand lens. However should gold be readily observed without a lens (or glass as it is often termed) then it is referred to as "V.G." meaning visible gold.

Figure 2-3: Checking a pan's contents

Fineness of Gold

Now this combining of gold with other metals, usually silver, will affect the purity of the placer gold. The purity of native gold is expressed in terms of fineness, meaning the proportion of pure gold within the sample as parts in 1,000. The fineness of placer gold varies from 500 to 999 (almost pure gold) while vein gold varies from 500 to 850. Most placer gold is about 800 fine. This means that the placer gold contains 80% of the element gold and 20% impurities. The latter is generally silver to a high degree, followed by copper, iron, zinc and lead in decreasing amounts. Now how does the R.V. placer miner tell the percentage of impurities in his placer gold? He can't without a chemical analysis. However the color of the recovered gold will give some indication of the amount of impurities. As the normal golden yellow sheen takes on a darker or more silvery look the impurities (with silver leading the pack) are increasing. This will have some effect on the revenue you will receive for your gold.

Extraction

The combining of gold, or melding, with other elements, led to the science of metallurgy, the art of extracting metals from their ores. The early proponents of metallurgy were the alchemists whose major preoccupation was the producing of gold from base metals. As sidelines, they endeavoured to find the elixir of life and the fountain of youth. The ancient miners probably separated native gold from other foreign matter in placer deposits by the settling or gravity approach. Little has changed as this is still the major process at placer showings. However the alchemists became metallurgists as more complex sulphide lode deposits were uncovered. An early discovery was the affinity of mercury for gold (amalgamation) and the separation by distilling the amalgam. In the 18th Century the chlorination method of gold extraction came into vogue but was eventually superseded by the discovery in the late 1800's of the cyanide process. This practice involves the dissolving of gold from a compound by a cyanide solution and the precipitation of the dissolved gold by the addition of zinc crystals. This approach still remains the dominating process in the milling of lode gold ores.

Now what does all this mean to the placer miner? He who journeys into strange places and pans for gold? These gold placers came into existence beginning with the erosion and break-up of the gold-quartz veins. As an example the relative density of gold means it will endure as a mineral, as opposed to breaking up, when the weathering elements start to work on its habitant (a quartz vein or as fine disseminations in lava or granite). Sure it will scratch as it is relatively soft. This scratching contributes to the amount of "fine" or "flour" gold found in placers. Its malleability and ductileness while assisting changes in shape will nevertheless prevent breaking up of the mineral. And finally specific gravity will often help isolate gold from the lighter minerals in the early stages of placer development. This latter property is one of the chief contributing factors in the commercial recovery of gold. In later chapters we will witness its use. Gold, one of the most captivating of metals, has occupied man's attention since antiquity. Its many chemical and physical qualities have brought about the art of metallurgy, the primary object of which is the isolation of the metal from its coupled condition. In placer mining we don't have to worry about metallurgy. We have the free gold!!

Now how did the placer gold get where it is? Let's go into more details.

Chapter 3

THE DEVELOPMENT OF A PLACER DEPOSIT

The term placer, which is derived from the Spanish, refers to a deposit of sand or gravel containing particles of a valuable mineral in sufficient quantity to be workable at a profit. Gold, tin, platinum and diamonds are the substances commonly won from placers. In spatial relations gold and platinum are worldwide, while tin is primarily placer mined in southeastern Asia and diamond placers are found along the west coast of Africa. We are principally interested in the search for gold.

The location of gold placers is a strong indication to the explorer that he is close to deposits of lode gold deposits. Placers have often been instrumental in giving clues to lode discoveries, and also in establishing gold mining districts.

Company, Family or Individual

Placer mining has appeal, because of the ease of discovery and the fact it is often the most profitable branch of the mining industry. The mining of gold is immune to the hazards which can affect other industries. The product is always in demand, cannot be overproduced, and has no competition. International economics, crises and intrigue will cause fluctuations in the price but there is always a ready market for the gold.

Placer mining is an operation that can be handled by an individual, a small group or a large concern. The amount of money invested in equipment dictates the return in gold metal. The daily panning by an individual of an auriferous stream can return values from $10 to $100 per day. A large company using sophisticated machinery can draw daily profits of $1000 to $3000. As stated the return is dictated by the energy, time and money expended, plus the gold content of the stream.

The writer is personally acquainted with a family who spend their summers placering a very productive stream in the Klondike. Their profits from three months work enables the elders to spend relaxing winters in a warm climate, and pay for a good university education for their three offspring.

So how does all this wealth accumulate and how do we get our share? First let us find out how placers are formed, then we'll learn how to test for them, finally ending up with what to do when we locate one!

Weathering and Disintegration

Gold placers are derived initially from the gold minerals embedded in gold quartz veins or mineralized rocks. The weather has a great effect on these formations. Rain, sun, wind, temperature — all these factors of weathering have their effect on the rocks, causing them to break up or disintegrate. This occurs over thousands of years. Other factors such as flowing water, frost, growth of vegetation, chemical action, and movement of the earth's crust all exert an influence on the process of disintegration.

The breakup of the gold-quartz veins, or the auriferous rock formations, frees the gold and the gangue minerals. Once weathering has completed its task, the transportation agencies move in and relocate the freed components.

Normally these quartz veins are on hillsides or atop ridges. The reason for these elevated locations is that quartz, the basic ingredient of veins is a hard mineral (remember it has a hardness of 7) and is most resistant to erosion. Consequently when weathering, over time, has worked its wonders on the rest of the hill the quartz vein is still standing out, but starting to break down. It is the last remnant of the original hill to go. So now we have a gold-quartz vein, or lode, badly broken up and rapidly being disintegrated. This is the origin of a placer deposit. Its eventual economic value as a placer will depend upon the transportation and accumulation of the gold particles in accessible areas.

Placer deposits lie either on surface or are buried. The surface deposits are the most accessible, consequently are the first to be depleted. They are the initial find in any placer gold rush. This type of deposit is well situated for an individual prospecting. It challenges the imagination and offers reward. However let's get back to the formation and types of gold placer bodies.

Arizona Placer

The particular condition related above existed when I visited a lode gold property north of Wickenburg, Arizona. Old time prospectors had located an outcropping of a quartz vein on top of a relatively flat mountain ridge. They had sank a shaft down some 130 feet on the vein before abandoning the property. Presumably the gold value they sought weren't there. The odd thing about this property was the amount of loose detrital quartz lying on the surface and spread downhill for 30 to 40 feet from the vein proper. My prospector guide said that during the Depression years, close-by neighbours would visit the property and pick up small nuggets of gold lying on the surface mixed with broken quartz. Unfortunately all visible gold nuggets had been collected! Two miles away at the foot of the mountain several large size placers were being worked on an active stream.

What I saw on top of the ridge was an uplifted placer deposit. The broken pieces of quartz-gold had been the boulders which lay on the bottom of an active stream. The area had undergone uplift and the top of the mesa had been eroded away to disclose the bottom of the old channel. Evidently the extensions of the river below the uplift could not be located.

Very fine gold will readily float on any liquid or might well be blown by the wind for any distance. Larger gold fragments need water volume and velocity to move them. Many times a disintegrated vein will spread down the slope of a hill. This phase is called eluvial, or hillside placer, which in reality, is a placer in transition. The gold, or heavy minerals, are "creeping" down the hillside towards a creek or gulch. This "creeping" is helped along its path by rain or snow melt and further assisted by a steep slope coupled with the heaviness (specific gravity) of the fragments. Eventually they reach a stream or rivulet which carries them the rest of their journey (alluvial deposit). See figure 3-1.

Erosion

How about the remainder of the hill or mountain which following the uplift was subjected to weathering followed by transportion? The break-up of these rock formations gives rise to the gravels, sands, and clays of the riverbeds. The gravels are the coarser fragments of rocks which because of their weight drop first out of the current, and rest on the bottom of the stream bed. The velocity of the current continues to push them along thus adding to the scouring of the stream bottom plus the rounding of these rock fragments into the traditional boulder shape. The scouring of the bed eats into the underlying rock formations and tends to break it up thus contributing to the ever deepening of the stream bed and, in addition, adding to the debris carried by the current.

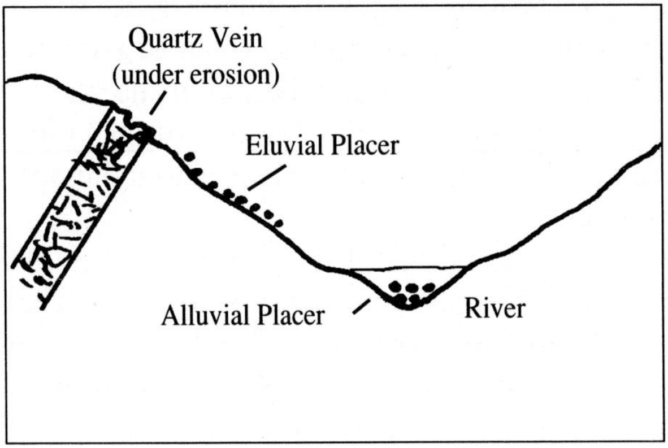

Figure 3-1: Placer in Transition

A stream, whether it is snow melt or surface water, gathers momentum as it comes down the mountain side and is generally joined by other rivulets or streams; all these tributaries adding to the volume of water being carried. These volumes of water carry solid debris such as gravels, sands and fines (clay) in addition to the heavier minerals gold, platinum, uraninite, galena, etc.

As the slope flattens out and the velocity of the current slackens, gravity takes over, certain heavy minerals and rock fragments drop out of the water to rest, or to be rolled along the stream bed. As the velocity continues to decrease the coarser fractions, gravels, etc., build up on the stream bed followed by finer debris, such as sand, being deposited above them. With the current now down to a very slow pace the finer fractions of the streams load are deposited as clay. Thus stratification has occurred with gravels on the bottom, through coarse to fine sands ending with clays near the top.

What is happening to the gold particles during all this activity? As I have stated gold has a heavy specific gravity and will eventually drop out of the stream's debris at the opportune time. As the larger cobbles start building on the stream floor, the coarser gold settles out of the main current and is lodged in the spaces between the boulders. With the slower flowing of the current the sands begin to settle and as the stream starts to slowly meander the fine gold is almost completely dropped — thus the stream has deposited its alluvial gold content. This surface deposit is the most common type of placer and the one most sought after.

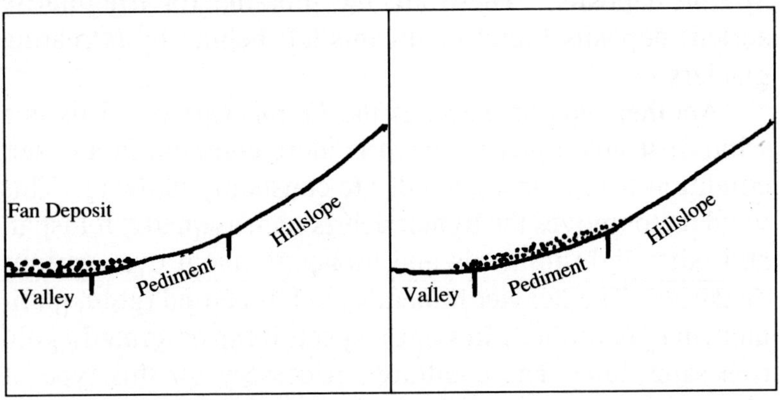

Figure 3-2: Gravel Deposits

Placer Types

The dry or desert placers of the southwestern states are known by the Spanish word *bajada*, meaning pediment. A pediment slope is a term commonly used in Nevada and Arizona with reference to ore locations, and is located on the lower portion of a desert hill where the slope flattens to 3° to 4° just prior to levelling into the valley bottom. See Figure 3-2.

They are formed in a fashion similar to stream placers, but the climate and topography of the desert makes for weak transportation of the debris. This weakness is caused by the decomposed debris being moved slowly down the canyons and washes, by wind and by the infrequent torrential floods. As this material reaches the bajada slope, the grade of the channel decreases and the water volume is dissipated into a ground seepage. The material is deposited on the slope or else moved further into the valley and deposited in the form of a fan as a gravel covered pediment (see Figure 3-2). Pediment placers are found at the foot of mountain ridges, within close proximity of the basin or valley.

Of slight interest to our particular area, are *Glacial Stream* deposits. These are the moraine (or irregularily sorted) deposits found in streams left behind by retreating glaciers.

Another type of placer is the *Eolian* variety. This is a wind distributed placer which is more common in a desert condition where strong winds are constantly blowing. This wind factor moves the lighter debris such as quartz, feldspar, and other light minerals and transports them over various distances. The heavier minerals are left behind (gold, platinum, magnetite etc.). In some respects it can be termed a gold rich sand dune. The conditions necessary for this type of placer are more common in the desert areas of Australia than in the southwest. Numerous eolian placers have been worked in the southern hemisphere.

Of importance in the Alaskan regions is a type of placer called *marine* or *beach placers*. These are formed by the sifting action of waves, undertows, and alongshore currents normally working against straight unbroken shorelines. Gold sources in these cases may be from bordering rocks, sediments deposited by emptying streams or rivers, or from auriferous terrace beds that line the coastline.

Figure 3-3: River Bar

Placer deposits are occasionally classified by their topographic locations. For example a *bench* or *terrace placer* (Figure 3-4) is a deposit left high on a present day hillside by an earlier stream. This stream was in some manner diverted or cut off so that its channel filled with gravel and the stream died. A later stream following the same pathway has eaten its way down through the gravels to the bedrock and continued through into the bedrock thus isolating the bench gravels lodged against the hillside.

River bar is an expression for a point in a river where it can be forded due to the projection of rocks close to the surface of the water. These rocks often accumulate heavy material on the upstream side. Depending on the velocity of the stream they can yield small amounts of gold. See figure 3-3.

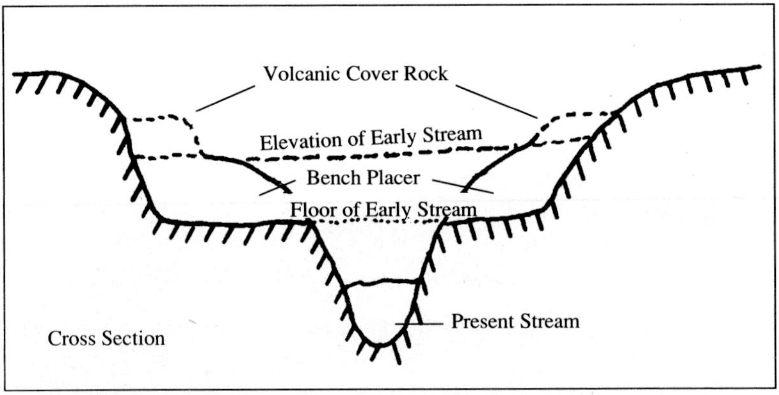

Figure 3-4: Bench Placers

A *gulch placer* is normally a shallow gravel deposit in a ravine which is subjected to periodic floods of rain. The term gulch is quite common in both desert and treed areas. In these areas transportation is very weak and non-continuous with the gold values likely coming from a nearby gold quartz vein.

A *gravel plain* is the spilling out of a stream's gravel load at its mouth due to the velocity decreasing as it enters a flat plain or valley. A delta is often formed in a similar manner but within a body of still water. Gold can be deposited in both delta and gravel plain placers.

Tertiary Placer Deposits

Up to now we've been discussing and illustrating how present day, or surface, placer deposits are formed. These surface placers have been formed over the last 100,000 years. The same processes must have gone on prior to this time. We can't go back *too* many eons in history because of the multitude of changes in physiography, environment and geomorphology.

At the beginning of the Tertiary era, a mere 65 million years ago, great changes were still being wrought on the physiography of the earth, particularly in the western half of North America. It was called the Laramide Revolution and was the last great mountain building era. The Rockies started to emerge and profound transformations took place along the Pacific coastal areas. During the latter part of the Tertiary period, the Alps and Himalayas rose from the sea floor, the Rockies and Andes reached their present height, mammals rose to dominance and Man emerged from the apes.

With the alterations in topography occurring over the Tertiary period, the streams associated with the mountains and valleys of the times, were often altered in their courseways. With the change in their flow movements the old channels became choked with the thick deposits of rapidly accumulating lean gravels, the detritus from weathering mountain slopes. Another cause of burial was capping from lava flows of active volcanoes.

Tertiary Potential

These buried channels are known as Tertiary channels because of the geological period of their birth. Todays changing landscapes have resulted in new river or stream channels being gouged out, often in the general area of the old, or Tertiary, channels. These new water runs have eroded canyons well below the elevation of the older buried channels.

The Tertiary channels are more in evidence in the Sierra Nevadas of California than in Nevada or Arizona. Some major Tertiary channels do exist in these states but the majority of these ancestral river systems flowed westward down the Sierra highland slopes to empty into a marine basin. A 1968 California mining report surveying the potential of that state's Tertiary gravels estimated the remaining reserves to total three to four billion cubic yards with an average grade of $2.50 per cubic yard (gold at $350/ounce) while zones in the lower sections of the gravels are estimated to contain 600 to 800 million cubic yards with an average grade of $10.00 per cubic yard. Based on these figures many major mining companies are investigating these Tertiary placers. The survey also estimated that some 1,600 million cubic yards averaging $3.20 per yard (gold $350) had been mined from the total reserve.

Recognition

How do we recognize these buried channels? One method of identification is *sidehill benches* (see Figure 3-4). As mentioned earlier the uplifting of an area with its stream beds choked with gravels of that era (Tertiary), allowed the present day waterways to follow the old watercourses while eating their way down to bedrock. This leaves part of the old riverbed exposed on the sidehill as a bench placer. Many times there are remnants of volcanic rock as cover over the bench. These bench placers often display the characteristic of a terrace, that is a relatively flat surface with a smooth slope on the creek side.

Sometimes following uplift there may not be any stream action on the old riverbed. However should erosion work on the cover of volcanic rock and strip it away, the underlying stream gravels may appear as a low gravel ridge. See Figure 3-5.

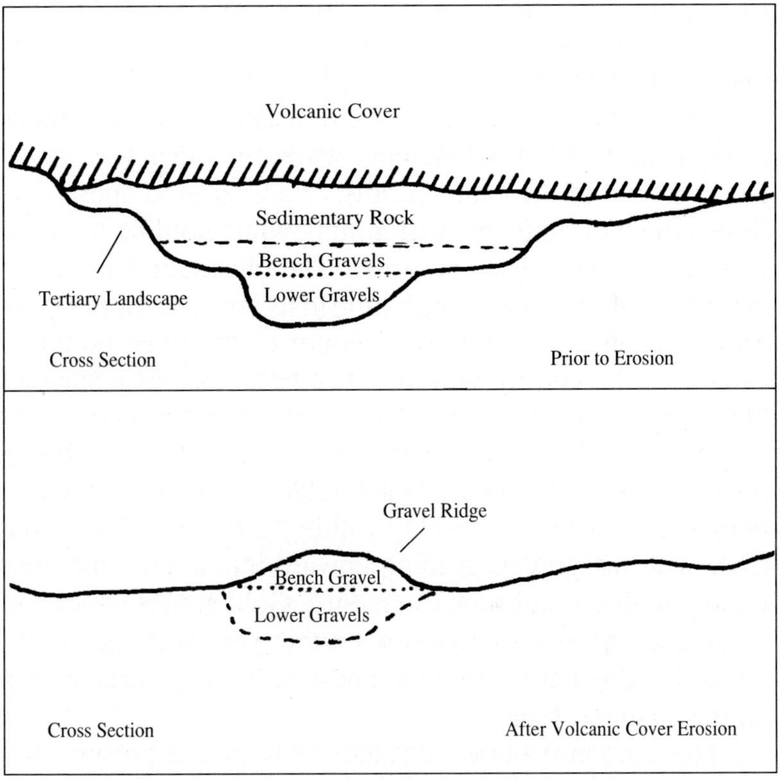

Figure 3-5: Erosional Effects on Bench Gravels

Should uplift not occur or fail to bring the buried placer bed completely to the surface, then resort must be made to geologic information available. In Chapter 'California', figure C-2, taken from studies of the ancestral rivers of the Sierra Nevada Range, shows the approximate outline of the buried streams to their present day water course. It will be noted that these Tertiary rivers flowed into an ocean which lapped at the foothills of the Sierra Nevadas.

Personally known to the writer is a buried placer operation some nine miles north of La Porte on the old Feather River Tertiary channel. Two vertical shafts were sunk through the surface volcanic cover and underlying gravels to bedrock. One shaft went to a depth of 140 feet while the second bottomed on rock at 250 feet. Obviously the latter was more in the centre of the old channel while the other was likely closer to one of the channel rims. Underground operations linked the two shafts by drift mining while holding the rock bed of the channel in the drift. The channel's rock floor demonstrated an undulating nature in its cross-sectional view probably due to the scouring nature of the huge boulders carried in the ancient current. The bedrock was a sheared black sediment called argillite. The lower gravels consisted of large boulders, with coarse gravel, resting on a badly broken rock floor. Some of the boulders exceeded three feet in diameter. The boulders lay within the first two feet of the floor with the gravels grading upward into a more medium variety with smaller rock fragments. Gold grades which ran as high as 0.15 ounces gold per cubic yard were generally located within a three foot thickness of those gravels resting on the channel floor.

The ancestral buried channel beds of the present day rivers have been relatively well located, particularly in the Sierra Nevadas. However, the mining of these beds is out of line for the RV prospector. Their inclusion in this chapter is for general information only, to expand your knowledge and to give you an overview of all placers and how they are formed.

Chapter 4

THE LOCATION OF GOLD PAY STREAKS

Now let's become familiar with paystreak deposition, before we learn the techniques of placer identification.

Generally, given an adequate primary gold source such as gold-quartz veins, the pay streaks will be fairly uniform. This condition will be maintained if the rainfall in the hilly country has been consistent and the uplift followed by erosion has been routine. However, any change in these standards will result in modifications to both the gold values and the continuity of the pay zone. Keep in mind there are rich and dry situations, so you will be well advised to try to locate these local pay streaks. No use staking the ground, then finding the pay streaks further up, or down, stream from your claim.

Pay streaks are fickle. There is no rule of thumb to define their location. Each type of placer produces its own peculiar streaks, and, as stated, any change in normal patterns provides variations in depositions.

High Grade Streaks

Wherever these gold streaks reside, whether gulches or young streams, they are generally easily located. They can usually be found lying close to bedrock in the grooves cut by the streams in a young valley (see Figure 4-1).This type of location requires removal of overlying gravels to get at these established pay streaks.

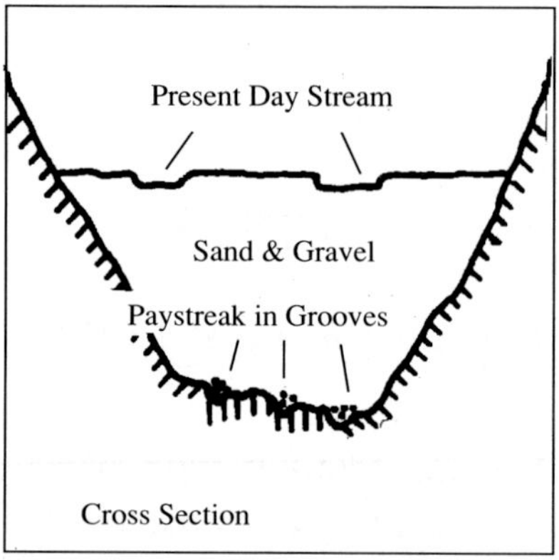

Figure 4-1: Paystreak at Depth

Now should a newly active stream, which is not necessarily following the old Tertiary water course, wear down through the gravels to the previously established pay streak, it would (where it crossed the old channel) pick up the earlier deposited gold, rework it into its load and deposit the reconcentrated material at convenient locations. This type of operation produces the richest pay streaks. A knowledge of where the present-day streams cross the old Tertiary channels will single out the most likely downstream location of a rich pay streak (see Figure 4-2).

Location Factors

What factors affect the pay streaks of present-day streams? The stream load, which includes the gravels and gold, is adversely affected by a slowdown in velocity. Where a tributary enters a stream, it contributes to the main stream's load. The tributaries' water velocity tends to overload the main stream's velocity, slowing it down slightly at that point and thus allowing some depositing of heavier load material (see Figure 4-3).

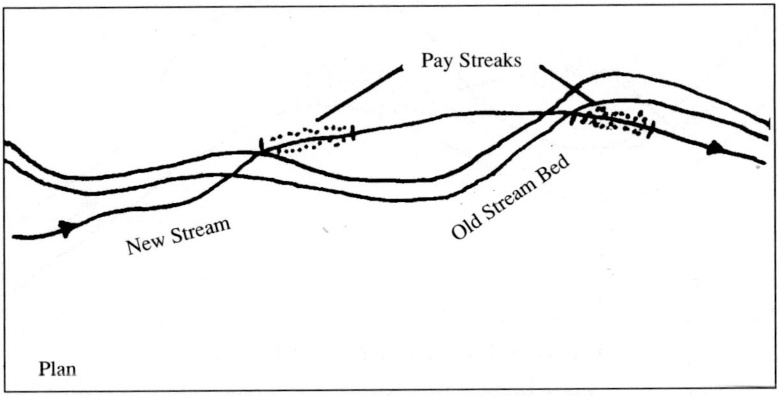

Figure 4-2: Likely Paystreak Location

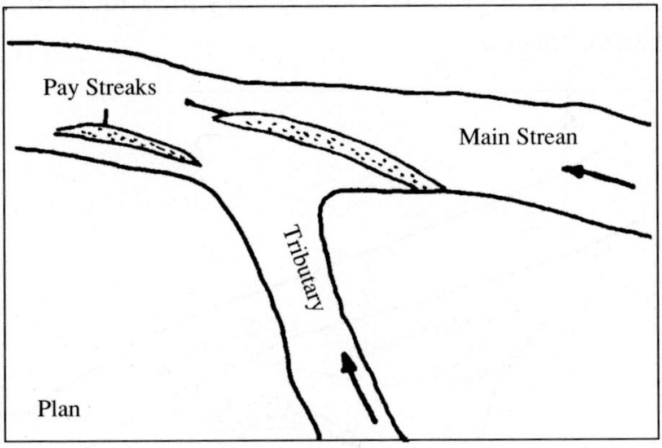

Figure 4-3: Junction Pay Streaks

A bend in a stream, such as that occuring prior to entering a large water body, or a meander in an older stream causes a slowdown in stream velocity, thus causing the stream to deposit its load; this occurs not on the cutting side of the meander but on that side building up (see Figure 4-4).

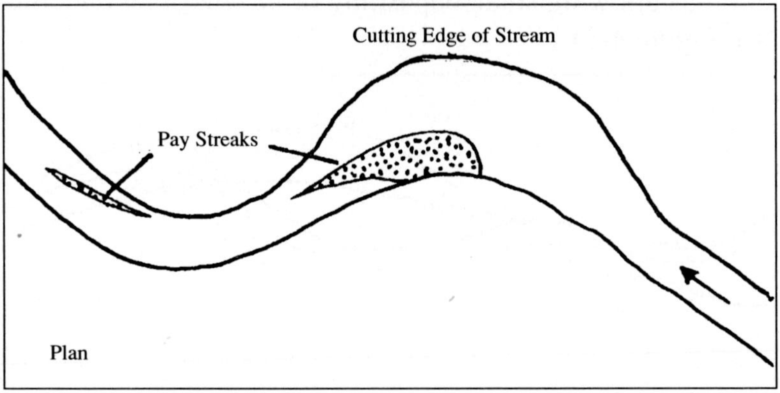

Figure 4-4: Pay Streaks in Meander

Streams meandering like this will often, if refreshed by additional water, straighten themselves out and leave meanders behind (see Figure 4-5). These dry meanders make good investigative targets.

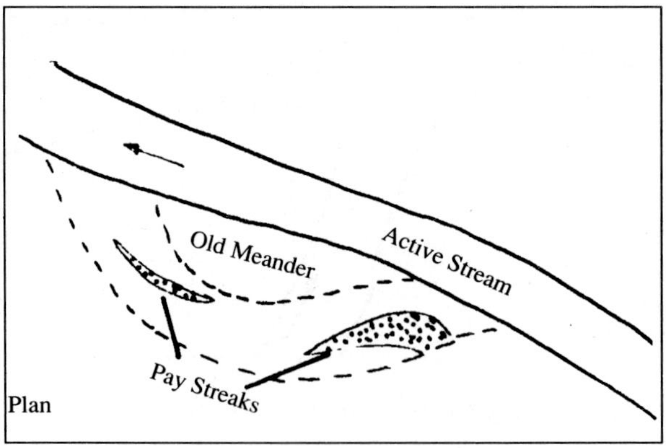

Figure 4-5: Dry Meander

Bedrock has an influence on pay streaks. Where the surface is uneven due to fracturing, the gold accumulates in the upstream side of the jutting rock or in depressions. This is due to the eddy currents that swirl in these locations (see Figure 4-6). This is a similar action to riffles in the bottom of the sluice box. Boulders, islands or other obstacles impede the progress of the water and cause a slowdown in velocity with subsequent deposition on the protected side.

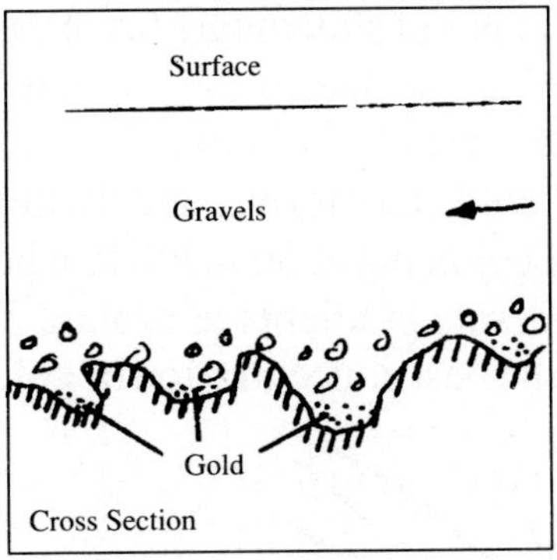

Figure 4-6: Gold Deposit on Uneven Bedrock

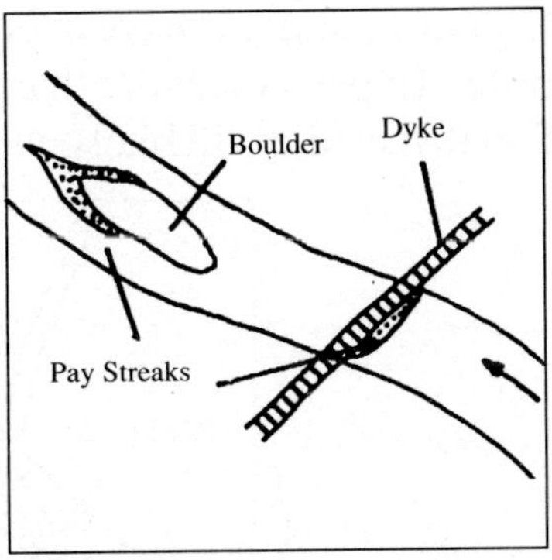

Figure 4-7: Pay Streaks at Obstructions

A resistant strata, such as a quartzitic dyke, cutting across a softer formation will act similar to uneven bedrock in a stream bed and cause a like buildup on the upstream side (see Figure 4-7).

Gold-quartz veins traversed by a stream will be water eroded and develop a pay streak downstream from the mineralized lode, as shown in figure 4-8. The early placer miners followed the trail of these rich pay streaks up-current to where they ceased, and then they looked around for the "mother lode". Many valuable deposits were found in this manner, particularily in the Sierra Nevadas.

Configurations

Pay streaks tend to be narrow and high grade. The upstream portion of a pay streak is normally made up of coarse gold which trails off downstream to finer gold. It is generally irregular in outline with branches and splits being commonplace. Little gold is found in whirlpools or rapids.

Neither the lower or upper reaches of streams are favorable locations for placer deposits. This is due to the stream's gradient effect on the velocity, which in turn affects the deposition of the gravels and gold. California and British Columbia streams have average gradients of 50 to 100 feet per mile. Experts consider that moderate gradients of around 30 feet to the mile will likely yield the best concentration of gold.

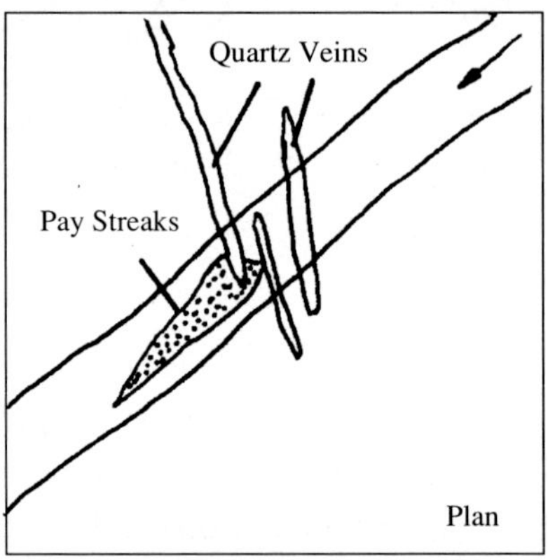

Figure 4-8: Paystreak Pattern After Quartz Vein

Gold Sizes

Most placer gold is in the form of fine flattened particle dust, very similar to the size of flaxseed. Nuggets are larger fragments, generally the size of a pea or walnut. But larger sizes are not uncommon. The finest particles of gold are called "flour" and is referred to as "colors" in the pan.

Desert Placers

In the more arid regions of Arizona and Nevada the gold is found in loose alluvium or wash in which no rounded pebbles exist. Usually the coarser gold is located at the head of the gulch, while the finer gold particles have been carried by wind or water further downstream (downgulch). The lack of pebble rounding is due to the irregularity of cloud bursts which flood the washes. There is no consistent water abrasion to smooth the pebbles. Poor water movement also contributes to a narrow pay streak.

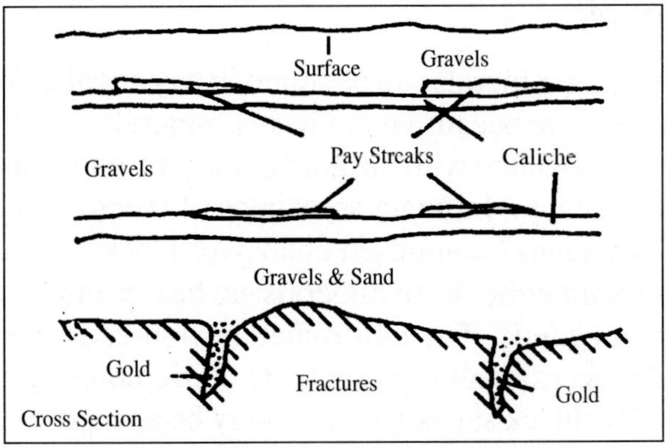

Figure 4-9: Placement of Gold on True and False Bedrock

Another feature of the desert placers is the elevation of the pay streaks within the gravels. They will appear at or near the true bedrock if it is at a shallow depth; oftentimes in this case, coarse gold will sift down to bedrock and become lodged, along with sand and gravel, in rock crevices. More often though, because of the lack of stratification in these dry placers, the pay streaks will appear at various higher levels usually associated with, or resting on, a layer of caliche. Caliche is a term given to gravel, sand, or desert debris (if it is at a shallow depth), cemented by porous calcium carbonate and which tends to form a series of false bedrocks. A similar situation to this exists in water-laid gravels where a "false bedrock" is generally compact clay beds within the gravels. It serves as a floor for placer gravels with other gold-bearing gravels possibly existing below (see Figure 4-9).

There is geological evidence showing an abundance of water in desert country. However, the water table is normally deeper than in more temperate climates. Many Arizona river beds have dry water courses with water running just a few feet below the surface.

Black Sands

What other minerals can be found in pay streaks? We know the gold is there because it is a heavy mineral; therefore other minerals associated with the gold in the pay zone must also be relatively heavy. Intimate associates of the gold deposit are the "black sands" composed chiefly of black magnetite and some dark ilmenite. Both minerals are heavy and magnetic to slightly magnetic, but unfortunately non-economic. Other minerals occasionally present are varicolored garnet and zircon. The black sands vary and may be as high as 98% of a paystreak.

Chapter 5

NECESSARY REQUIREMENTS

Like any good professional, gold seekers require that proper attire and equipment be part of the search. No plumber or carpenter worthy of their profession would go out on a job without the proper tools; the same applies to the week-end prospector or R.V. recreational miner. To equip yourself for this experience does not require an extensive or expensive layout, but it does require that certain tools both for safety and for the search become part of the field dress.

I will list the requirements and elaborate on the necessity and use of each item. They are: compass, gold pan, geological pick, vials or containers, tweezers, magnet, small magnifying glass, insect repellent, shovel, and maps of the area.

Compass

If you are going to wander off any roadway into the bush or across a desert, a compass is an absolute necessity. They can be purchased for prices ranging from $15 up to $250 from most rock or mining supply stores. Don't go too cheap on a compass — it can save your life should you get lost! There are some Swedish compasses on the market at around $45 that are ideal for this type of venture. The instructions that accompany the compass are comprehensive and should be read carefully. Also several "dry runs" or "shots" should be taken by the would-be woodsman prior to hitting the trail. More expensive compasses such as the Brunton ($200 - $250) are available for those who plan to go further afield from recognizable landmarks.

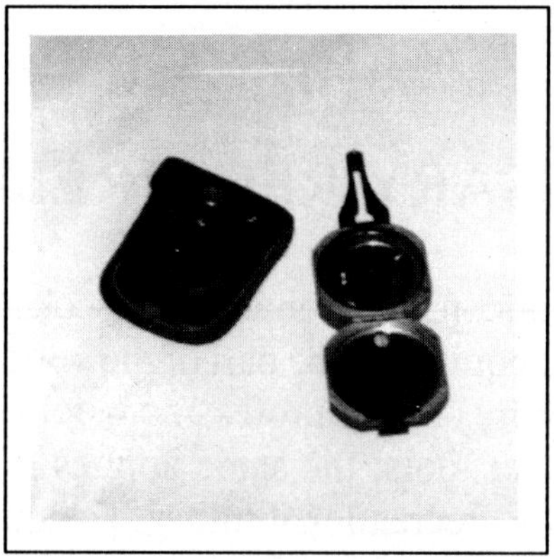

Figure 5-1: Brunton Compass

Compasses are used in conjunction with "declination" bearings. In the northern hemisphere, the compass needle is attracted by the magnetic north pole, which is approximately 800 miles south of the true north pole. Therefore the angle between the north pole and the magnetic pole from the observer's location is referred to as the magnetic declination. This is expressed in degrees either east or west of true north. All topographic, geographic and geologic maps show their declination angle which, when operating in this particular map area, must be added or subtracted to the compasses' readings. Instructions will show how to embody this in the use of the compass. The writer would recommend purchasing a 360° azimuth compass as opposed to a quadrant compass.

Gold Pan

The gold pan is a flat-bottomed, circular dish usually made of steel or iron although copper or aluminum are also available. The pan is shallow, about 2 1/2 to 3 inches deep, with an inside slope of 30°. The upper surface of the pan is usually 16 inches across but can vary from 15 inches to 18 inches . The rim is turned back for ease of handling. In weight they seldom exceed 5 pounds. They can take a lot of abuse but should be discarded if punctured.Lately pans of high impact plastic are available. Their durability and light weight make them very popular. I personally like this type of pan.

Figure 5-2: Placer Pan

The cost of a pan varies from $5 to $15. Each R.V. prospector should have at least two. Ensure that they are free of oil or grease at all times.

Geological Pick

This, like the compass, should be considered standard gear. The pick is useful for chipping rocks, breaking up hardpan or caliche before it enters the gold pan and for prying into rock crevices. It resembles a normal nail hammer with one end being the flat striking surface while the other end is either chisel-like or pointed. Normally the shank and head are cast as one, but a wooden handle is available. My personal preference is the pointed tip, all steel construction with a rubber shank grip, weighing 20 ounces. Prices vary between $20 and $35. It is advisable when rock chipping to wear safety goggles.

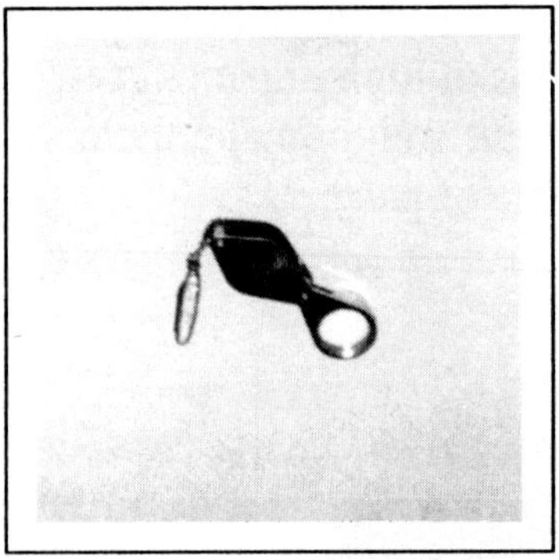

Figure 5-3: Magnifying Glass

Figure 5-4: Geological Pick

Vials or Containers

These are required after panning a suspected gold stream with the resulting gold concentrate or black sands. The panned product is placed in the vial (plastic or glass) for further upgrading at a later time. They are also useful for classifying the gold flakes as they pass through different screens. For example, one vial could be tagged as "nuggets", another "10-20 Mesh, Medium Gold", while a third could be labelled "Fine Gold, 20-40 Mesh", while a fourth would be labelled "Very Fine Gold, Passes 40 Mesh". See Appendix-Mesh Sizes. Classified in this manner makes for easier sales, in addition to spectacular display purposes. Vials are obtainable at any mining outlet, hardware store or pharmacist supply house. It is suggested that large jars be obtained for the storage of the black sand prior to final concentration of the gold.

Tweezers

The normal 4 3/4 inch tweezer with smooth points is very handy for picking grains of gold out of the gold pan. They can be purchased for a modest sum at any drugstore.

Magnet

This is an important item, particularly when panning has come up with a fair amount of black sands and contained colors. As the black sands are highly magnetic, large amounts can be pulled out of the gold pan by running a strong magnet under the pan, attracting the black sands and leading them to the pan's edge where they can be scraped away. Don't put the magnet down in the sands, as you might well be spending the rest of your holiday removing the sands from the magnet. The plastic gold pans are particularly good for this purpose as the metal pans have a tendency to attract and make moving the magnet a difficult job.

It is recommended that a high power magnet be purchased. There are some small efficient magnets with a pull force of 25 pounds available in the $20 to $25 range.

Magnifying Glass

A good magnifier serves several purposes to the weekend prospector. It will readily allow identification of gold colors in a pan concentrate and also permit good examination of minerals in a rock sample. The magnifier is strictly an aid to our vision. Don't sacrifice width and depth of field for the sake of magnification. A good 16 power glass will allow sufficient magnification to identify objects without having to move the glass at short increments over the study field.

Glasses can be purchased from 6 to 20 power. At the latter intensity the field is so confined and the depth so restricted that identification becomes an involved procedure. Prices start around $25 working up to $45 depending on the magnification.

Shovel

This is an important item to work with the gold pan. Dry or wet gravels must be dug from a gulch or a creek bed. It is recommended that a small spade-type shovel be obtained, preferably one that folds for convenient carrying. If the operation expands from the pan to the rocker or similar unit then the supply to the unit is increased and we are looking at a two person operation, one digging, the other handling the rocker or sluice.

Maps of the Area

These can be obtained from the Geological Surveys of the various states, from a local University or from a map supply store in the region. You will need to have a good road map,plus either a topographic, geographic or geologic map of the area. The topographic map will show elevation contours, along with permanent and intermittent streams plus paths or trails of the area. The geographic maps identify local landmarks but do not, as a rule, show the relative steepness of mountains or canyons. The stream tributaries which gush at certain times of the year are not always identified. Geologic maps show the different rock stratae of the area as mapped by the Geologic Survey. They will be of interest to the advanced RV prospector who knows the most logical type of rock to have (or had) gold quartz veins contained within that formation.

The maps can be obtained in quadrants, normally 2 degrees in width, which cover an extensive area. Prices range from $1 to $5.

Gold Balance

I hesitated before including this item because of the cost involved. A good portable balance of the type used in weighing gold can run $250 and upward. It is a very good item to have especially if you are working a productive gold stream or gulch. At the end of the season you can total your take in ounces and know your prospective revenue.

Mercury

This is a chemical requirement if you are concentrating your gold by a method known as amalgamation. Further reference will be made to this method in later chapters. The mineral is not cheap selling at pharmaceutical suppliers or mining retailers for around $14.50 per pound. However it is recoverable for further use. Be aware it is a very poisonous mineral and, environmentally, it is frowned upon.

Insect Repellent

This is a must especially during the fly season. Carry a good brand of repellent when you are panning along a stream where flies and mosquitoes are annoying.

The above products are an integral part of a gold panning adventure. Now should you intend to prospect further afield, that is, into the wilds away from the highways, the material requirements increase. With no comments on these necessities, I herewith list some of the dispensables and the indispensables.

(1) A nylon tent, size dependent on number of people.
(2) Good leather or rubber boots.
(3) First Aid kit, including snake bite antidote.
(4) Comfortable nylon sleeping bag.
(5) Head covering of some nature (To keep sun and insects off).
(6) Small hatchet.
(7) Matches in waterproof container plus candles.
(8) Salt pills.
(9) Field notebook plus pencils.
(10) Shrill whistle.
(11) Signal mirror (if not on compass)
(12) Miscellaneous material for survival such as fishing line, extra high energy food over and above normal rations.

All this equipment plus food will pack nicely into a large backpack with either the tent, canvas, or sleeping bag riding on top. Practice packing a few times before you set off.

Needless to say if striking out on your own, have a good topographic map indicating trails, and outline in advance your intended trip. Above all, advise someone else where you intend to go in the event that you should become delayed or lost and when you expect to return.

Oh, one last word! In today's environmentally-conscious society *please* leave your campsite clean when you depart.

Chapter 6

THE INITIAL APPROACH

So now we know *what* we are looking for, and also, when we arrive at our destination, just *where* we should look. What preparations should we be making?

Let's presume you are RVing in the Prescott area (the chapter on Arizona placers lists several known placer prospects in this area). Suppose you pick the Black Canyon area. The text states it can be reached without leaving the road. Upon reaching the location you find a smooth flowing stream with some ramblings in its course. Pick an area where it appears the streams flow has been decreased due to impediments in the water course as suggested in Chapter 4. Check the availability of gravels, get out the gold pan and shovel, and get ready for action.

First let's learn the technique of gold panning. It is not a stringent process but it is back breaking. This results from squatting and bending as you search along the creeks edge. It can also be boring until colors start appearing in your pan, that's when the adrenalin starts to flow.

Basically, panning and other procedures, such as rockering and sluicing is a method of reducing gravel bulk to an amount where more intense treatment becomes economically viable. The resultant mixture is termed a concentrate.

There are two types of panning: wet panning,that done along creeks or stream beds and dry panning that carried out in dry washes or desert gulches. The former is the most common so we will start from there.

Steam (Wet) Panning

The mechanism of concentration in a pan is very similar to a gravity concentration and involves some four mechanical steps, incorporating four processes. The processes include 1) Sizing— that is arranging the material in a rather loose fashion, with the bigger and heavier fractions on the bottom of the pan; 2) Suspension—that is taking the lighter material up into the liquid (water) and maintaining in this floating state; 3) Stratification— the heavier grains due to their weight, settle down in the bed of the material overcoming the density of the pan material; 4) Film sizing—that is the elimination of material from the pan according to their weight, starting with the more coarse material and working down to finer sands. So much for the theory of panning, now let us learn the operation.

A normal gold pan holds from 15 to 28 pounds of gravel material. It is recommended that the load be no greater than 20 pounds in order to allow ease and duration, to the operation. Gold gravel weights 3300 pounds to the cubic yard, therefore 165 pans of material equals one cubic yard. Load your pan with material from the area you are investigating, then

1) Submerge the pan in water. While under water, work the gravel over gently with the hands all the while removing any large pebbles or rocks. Continue until all large material has been removed, and all clay, or cemented gravels, have been broken down.

2) While still under water hold the pan horizontal and begin a rotary motion to the pan. The lighter material will carry into suspension while the heavier material including the gold particles will work toward the bottom of the pan.

3) Bring the pan above the water and tilt it slightly away from you while rocking the pan from side to side. This results in solid material being washed to the lower tilted edge. Be careful to ensure that only the surface material gathers at the tilted rim.

4) The accumulated material is now washed off by alternately dipping and raising the pan through the waters surface and is further aided by gently pushing the gathering material off with the thumb.See figure 6-1.

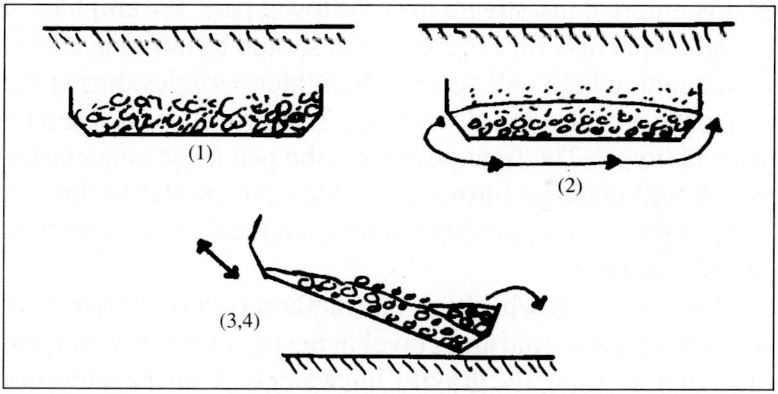

Figure 6-1: Panning Procedure

Keep repeating these operations until material remaining in the pan is small and consists of heavy dark minerals mixed with slight amounts of fine light sands. This is your concentrate and should be stored in a large plastic container for further separation back at your RV. Final separation is by magnetic methods, amalgamation and retorting, or centrifuge.

Any small nuggets which have shown up by this time should be removed and stored in a special jar. The same goes for colors which appear during the panning procedures. Pick these gold colored particles out of the gravel with your tweezers and store in a small plastic vial. So much for wet panning.

Desert (Dry) Panning

Dry panning is often called winnowing, and involves the use of two gold pans. The gravel, with the larger boulders removed by hand, is placed in one pan. The other empty pan is placed on the ground and the full pan, at shoulder height, is gently emptied in a stream over the lower pan. We emphasize a slight wind or a breeze from a fan should be blowing across the stream, which will deflect the lighter particles during the fall to the outside of the lower pan. This procedure is repeated several times. The final product in the pan is the concentrate which will undergo further concentration similar to the wet concentrates. Dry panning is slower and more uncertain than the wet method.

One of the drawbacks of this method is the differences in density between gold and gravel in the mediums of water and air. Air has no specific gravity, but water is given the reference figure of 1. Therefore the ratio in *air* between gold (19.3 specific gravity) and quartz gravel (2.65 specific gravity) is 19.3 divided by 2.65, or 7.28. However, if immersed *in water* the ratio becomes (19.3 - 1) divided by (2.65 - 1) or 11.09. This means that gold in water (wet panning) is eleven times heavier than the gravel, whereas in air (dry panning) gold is only seven times heavier than gravel. Almost $^2/_3$ of an increase in the specific gravity (or weight) when water is used.

The Concentrate

OK you've put in some 10 hours of steady gold panning. You have run through some 60 pans of gravel: that is 6 pans per hour, or one every 10 minutes. Once you become proficient you should be able to run through some 100 pans in 10 hours of normal gold gravels. The reason for this calculation will become clearer later as we calculate your daily profit.

Let's presume that from each pan you end up with 2 - 8 ounces of black sand concentrates. This means at the end of the day you have some 10 to 40 (troy) pounds in total. This must be dried. Spread it out on a fine cloth and either artificially dry it with a hair dryer, or allow it to dry overnight.

Next day while you are out panning, a member of the family can magnetically get rid of the black magnetite in the heavy sands. There are many approaches, one being placing a magnet under a cloth containing the "cons" and moving the black magnetic material to the edge, then on to paper. This then leaves a concentrate of black non-magnetic minerals, light colored sands, and gold on the cloth. At this stage it is likely you can remove the larger gold flecks by means of a tweezer. Once the magnetic portion of the dry concentrate has been removed it is recommended that the remaining amount be spread *very* thin on a large piece of paper. Using a hair dryer at its lowest speed, direct it across the material thereby whisking away additional grains of sand and black mineral and leaving gold behind.

Should you build up a quantity of gold with slight amounts of sand, sizing, using a series of coarse to fine mesh screens (20 - 100 mesh), will help to eliminate much of the sand, and also sort the gold into their respective sizes.

Amalgamation

Gold can best be amalgamated with mercury in the concentrated form. I recommend that much of the magnetic portion of the heavy sands be removed prior to amalgamation. Place approximately 5 pounds of concentrate in a gold pan and add roughly one ounce of mercury to the material. Agitate the contents under water in a tub until the mercury takes up all the visible gold. Now, as before, pan the remaining sands away while retaining the amalgam (gold plus mercury) and the unused mercury in the pan. The next step is retorting to free the gold from the mercury.

Prior to retorting, check if the gold amalgam has an excess of mercury. If so place the amalgam in a canvas or muslin bag and allow the mercury to drain overnight into a dish. To recover even more, gently squeeze the bag.

To separate the gold from the amalgam now requires retorting. This means heating the amalgam to produce a gaseous mercury, then cooling this vapor to condense it into the liquid mercury with the residual material remaining in the pot containing gold.

It is recommended that if the RVer intends to retort his amalgam, that he purchase the amalgam retort equipment from a chemical or mining equipment supplier. Prices range from $60 up. The three components of a retort are 1) Container with tight lid (amalgam holder) 2) A condenser pipe (to convert the gas to purified liquid mercury) 3) Collection dish (to gather purified liquid mercury). Figure 6-2 illustrates the set-up for retorting.

PRECAUTIONS

Several points should be emphasized concerning the retorting of the amalgam. The operation should take place in a well ventilated room or, preferably, out in the open. Mercury vapors are very poisonous. Fill the container only half full. Make sure the lid is *tightly* secured. Keep the burner flame under the container low at first, then gradually build up to a medium flame.(Complete retorting instructions are contained in Chapter 8.) If you prefer, the amalgam may be shipped to an assay lab for the separation.

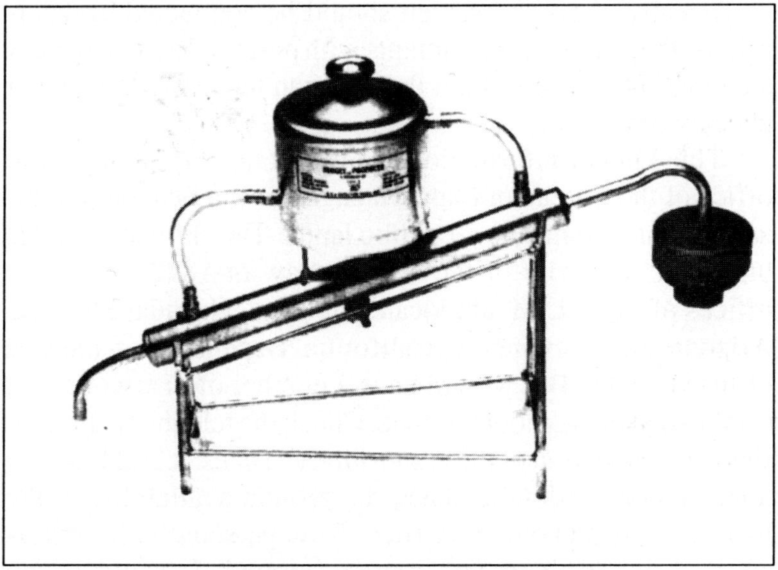

Figure 6-2: Nugget Retort Setup

A unique method which I have not employed, involves cutting in half a large firm potato, hollowing a large hole in the centre of one half, filling the hole with amalgam, pressing and tightly sealing the two halves together, then burying in the coals of a campfire for one hour. The resulting product is said to be a gold button. Some recoverable mercury can be squeezed out of the potato pulp. Needless to say the poisonous potato should be incinerated!!

Checking the Ground

Well here we are: we have recovered a certain amount of gold from a stream, so what happens now? If there is enough gold to give you the feeling that this could be *your* dream stream then the next step is to check ownership of the particular area. No point trying to acquire, or work the ground, if someone else has a legal claim to the property.

Locally a ground search should be conducted to determine if there are any monuments with notices, as used to mark a claim, in evidence. If not then we can move onto the paper check work.

This kind of information can be obtained from any local office of the Bureau of Land Management, a Federal organization which manages all public lands. The Bureau operates under the authority of the Mining Law of 1872. The State offices of the B.L.M. are located in Reno, Nevada; Phoenix, Arizona, and Sacramento, California. Depending on the size of the state, the B.L.M will have a number of district offices established throughout the state. Check the telephone directories for the location of these subsidiary offices. It is also sound management to double check the ground availability at the local County Recorder's Office. Now personally, in preference to doing all of this running around, I would (if no evidence exists of prior staking) establish my own claim to the ground by staking it, then go to the nearest B.L.M *and* County Recorder's office to record the claim(s). If at this point it becomes apparent that someone else has prior claim to the ground, forget about recording your claim. Unless the ground has been patented or is private property there should be some physical evidence (claim monuments, drill test sites, equipment etc.) that the ground belongs to someone else.

Now there being no evidence of other ownership of the ground let us first understand what a "claim" is, then prepare to stake our "claim" to the property. A claim is the portion of mining ground held under Federal and local laws by one individual, or a group of individuals (association) by virtue of one location (staking) and recording. No licence is required to stake claims in the U.S. but the locator of the mining claim must be an American citizen or one who has declared his intention to become a citizen of the U.S. There are no restrictions regarding age, sex, or residence of the locator. A corporation organized in any state, a partnership, or two or more qualified persons can locate a claim. An agent can locate a claim for any qualified person, group, partnership or corporation even though the agent might not be qualified to locate a claim for himself. Incidentally, there is no limit to the number of placer claims that can be staked, but a valid discovery must be made on each claim. An individual or company can stake a single placer claim of 20 acres. An association can stakes a 20 acre claim per individual number of people within the association. For example 4 people can have an 80 acre placer claim, to a limit of 8 people (160 acres).

There are certain areas where staking is not permitted. These reserved areas are Federal and State parks, National Monuments, Indian reservations, established wilderness areas, the beds of navigable lakes and streams, military reservations, granted railway sections, and certain National Wildlife Refuges and Recreation areas.

On privately owned land, the mineral rights must be obtained from the owner either through purchase or lease.

Procedures of Location

The previous paragraphs referred to the do's and don'ts of staking. Now let's check the procedure for obtaining a placer claim. I'll list the general steps then elaborate on each operation:

1) Make a valid discovery of a valuable mineral deposit.
2) Erect a location monument at the point of "discovery".
3) Prepare a notice of location for each claim and post it on or in the monument.
4) Erect corner monuments and mark out the boundaries (within 60 days), unless the claim is taken by legal subdivision .
5) Record within 90 days the claim location. After the 90 day period the claim is null and void if not recorded.

The above 5 steps will make you the owner of a legal placer claim(s). To elaborate:

1) *Valid Discovery*: Emanating from the original 1872 Mining Act the courts have established that the "discovery" is to be subjected to the "Prudent Man" test. To explain, this means that a prudent man of limited means would spend money on the discovery if he saw future production possibilities in the deposit. Since the early 1970's the marketability aspect has been combined with the Prudent Man approach.

If you are staking a placer claim along a creek or in a dry gorge, then due to your prior panning of the material and subsequent discovery of gold you can be confident of recording a discovery. From this standpoint alone, placer claims are more subject to fall into the true meaning of "discovery" than lode claims. The marketing of placer gold is never in doubt.

2) *Location Monument:* A placer claim has dimensions 1320 feet in length (normally along the course of the stream), and 660 feet in width, thus encompassing 20 acres. A location monument is placed along the north boundary at any point. See figure 6-3.

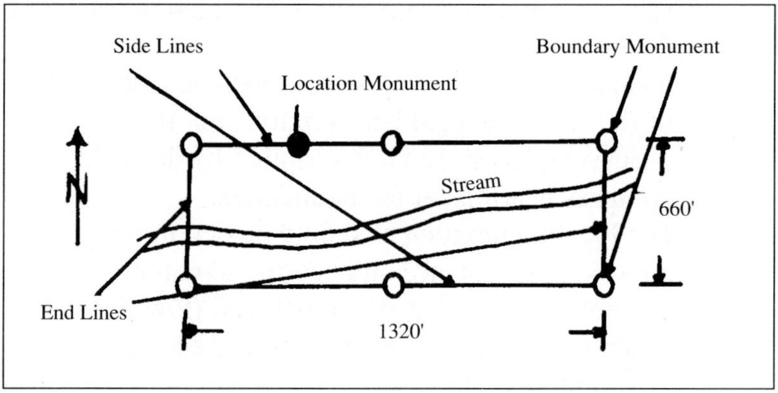

Figure 6-3: Locating a Placer Claim

This monument can be:

a) A cut tree three feet in height, 4 inches through the butt and squared at the top.

b) A 4" by 4" wooden post , a 3" diameter PVC piping, or a metal pipe all protruding 3' above the ground.

c) A rock cairn 2 1/2' to 3' in height.

The PVC piping is proving very popular with stakers, particularly in desert conditions due to their lightness in handling.Figure 6-7.

3) *Notice of Location:* This notice is a written piece of information detailing the claim and is posted on or in the location monument. It can be placed in a plastic bag and nailed or clipped to the monument or inserted in a can and placed in the rock cairn. The writing should be legible and non-fading. It should be sheltered from the elements. It is your notice to others that this claim has been located by you. The notice should state:

a) Name of the claim. Type of claim.

b) Name and post office address of locator.

c) Date of location.

d) Number of acres claimed

e) The mining district and county in which the claim is located.

f) If in a surveyed area, it should include a description of the claim by legal land subdivision. If in unsurveyed area then a description by distance and compass bearings of the boundaries.

g) The location monument should be tied in by approximate distance and bearing to natural (mountain peaks, rivers) or artificial (towns, roads) landmarks, which points will be marked on government maps.

A copy of this Notice of Location is found in the Appendix.

Figure 6-7: Claim Monuments

4) *Mark out the Boundaries:* At each corner of the claim a monument must be built. In addition, another monument must be located midway along both side lines which are the longer (1320') sides of the boundary. No midpoint markers are required along the end lines (660').

If the claims are being staked in desert conditions, the above are the only requirements, as normally line of sight allows the complete claim to be seen from any monument. If staking in a treed area, it is best to mark the boundary by "blazing" trees or stringing colored ribbons from the branches along the route.

"Blazing" means slicing (by an axe) the bark of the tree to a shallow depth to produce a visible mark approximately 8" x 3" at eye level. No harm is done to the tree and the route is marked.

It is required by law that the boundaries of the placer claim be established within 60 days of locating the claim. It is good policy to erect the boundaries and put in the monuments at the time the claim is being located.

An essential is that the location monument be located on 'open' ground, meaning not previously staked by someone else, whereas the boundary monuments can be located on staked ground. If you are locating inside an area previously staked, the ground legitimately claimed is that which does not overlap the prior location. See sketch 6-4.

If in surveyed territory, Federal mining law requires that a placer claim conform, within reason, to the system of public land surveys and be located as part of the survey coordinates. See Figure 6-5. That is, its boundaries should be north-south and east-west if possible. Incidentally if you are locating within surveyed territory, you will only require a location monument.

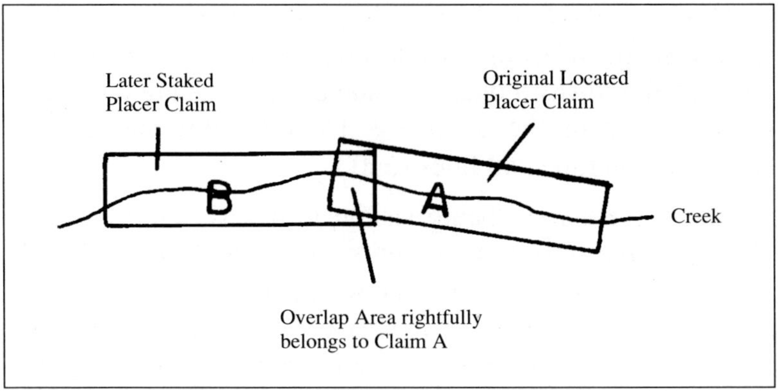

Figure 6-4: Disputed Area in Overstaking

5) *Recording*: Within 90 days, record at the local county recorder's office *and* the State office of the Bureau of Land Management a true copy, and duplicate of the Certificate of Location for each claim, along with two copies of a map of the claim, or group of claims. The Certificate of Location should contain all the data you have placed on the Notice of Location. The map should show the relationship of the claim to the public land survey, or if in unsurveyed township, it should be related to a readily identifiable landmark. In addition the map must describe the position of the boundary monuments in relation to each other, and establish numbers for each of these monuments. Also the map should contain:

a) Type of claim (placer or lode)
b) Name of claim
c) Date of location
d) Name and address of locator
e) The county
f) Type of monument
g) Bearing and distance between monuments

h) Scale of map
i) A north arrow (true or magnetic)
See Figure 6-6.

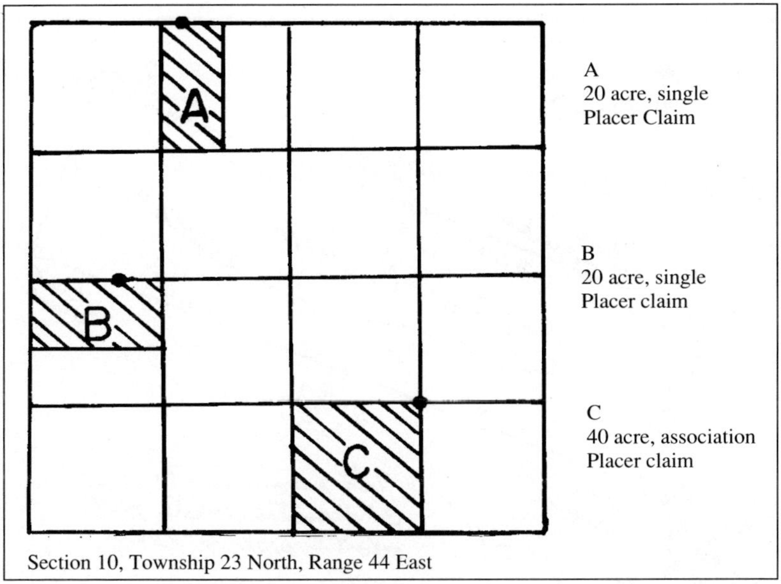

Figure 6-5: Staking in Surveyed Township

Do ensure that the proper procedures are followed. If your notices, monuments and recording are in proper order you will have no trouble in receiving that ground which you located. However do check the area to be sure that you are not staking somebody else's ground. Nothing can be more embarassing than to be informed at the BLM office, or the county recorders office, that the ground already belongs to someone else!

Now if all this seems intimidating, don't be alarmed. Like all government rules the precautions are there for your protection. Again it is learning something new and the routine must be undergone. Once the first location has been completed and the filings dispensed with, it will be like "old hat" from there on.

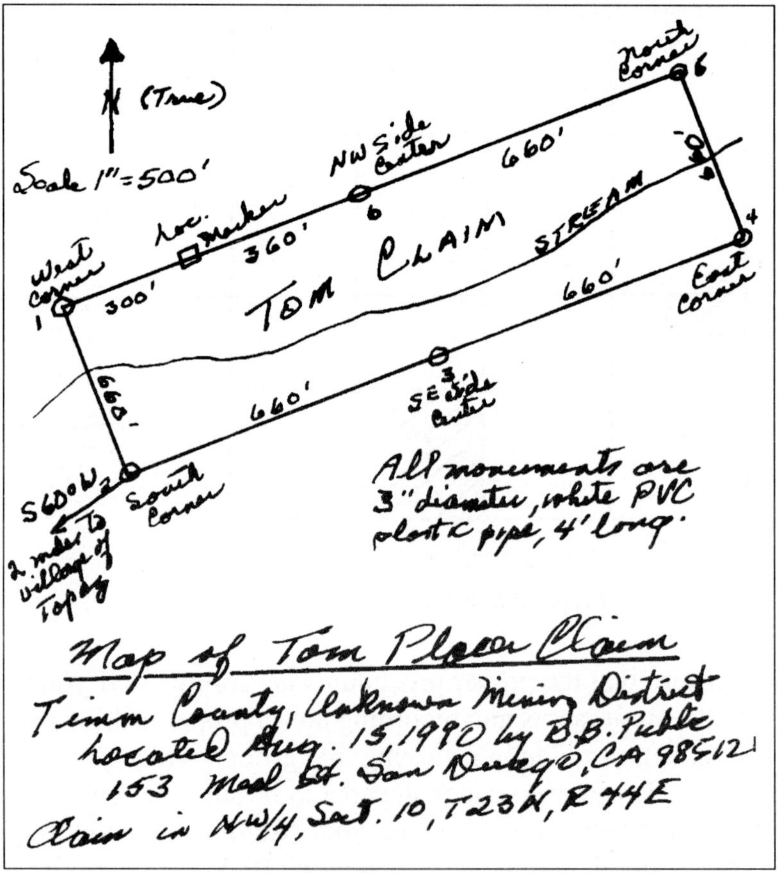

Figure 6-6: Type of Map to Accompany Certificate of Location

Chapter 7

MOVING INTO HIGH GEAR

We have now arrived at the point where decisions must be made. We have found a stream that has given us some indications of gold. We have checked the files of the local County Recorder's Office and the State Office of the Bureau of Land Management, and made sure that there are no claims filed on our stream. We have staked and claimed our 20 acre claim. Now it is ours — all ours !!

Now what do we do? We have several choices:
1) Hold the claim on an annual basis, visit when we want, and pan as much as we want. This is a leisurely approach, particularly suited to a nice location where we can RV close by and settle down to a relaxing (and hopefully subsidized) holiday.
2) We can take a more serious approach, which will mean more equipment, time and expenses.

The Choices

Taking the first approach means you can now relax, enjoy the countryside, do your occasional panning, refine the concentrate, and make the most of a nice situation. Oh, a word — don't forget to do your annual assessment on the claim. More about this in a later chapter.

However, making the second choice means setting up a modest size operation (a Mom & Pop operation if you will). So let us look at the economics of small and medium operations. See figure 7-1.

Figure 7-1: Family Operations

Small is panning and processing say 80 pans a day. A medium operation is machine run at a minimum of a cubic yard per hour or 10 cubic yards per day. For contrast, the more aggressive mining companies look at a volume of 200 yards per day, or even per hour!

In placer mining, the reference to volume is normally in bank yards which is a packed cubic yard of gravel. Placer mining involves gravel, referred to as unconsolidated sediments by geologists. The weight of a bank yard of pure sand is 2700 pounds while gold-gravel is accepted as 3300 pounds to the bank yard due to the bouldery nature of the gravels.

At analytical laboratories, values of precious metals (gold, silver and platinum) are given in ounces per ton. When placer mining, we must convert the value per ton to value per bank yard. When we do this we will always come up with a higher value figure because we will be changing from 2000 pounds (per ton) to 3300 pounds (per cubic yard).

As an example of conversion, say an analysis by a chemical laboratory gives a gold value of 0.05 ounces gold per ton. The mathematics becomes

$$\frac{0.05}{2000 \text{ (Weight Per Ton)}} \times 3300 \text{ (Weight Per Yard)} = 0.0825 \text{ oz. Gold per Yard}$$

Now to go back to our panning. If the value of the gravels assayed at 0.0825 ounces gold per bank yard, then at the 1991 average price per ounce of gold ($350 U.S.), this will give a dollar value of $28.88 per bank yard to the gravels.

So if you have panned down 80 pans you could have an average of, say, 10 pounds of concentrates (black sands and gold) that you have lovingly labored over all day. This from 80 pans, of 20 pounds average, for a total throughput of 1600 pounds. This gives a ratio of concentration of 1:160, meaning 1 part concentrate from every 160 parts gravel. However you did not pan a full bank yard, only 1600 ÷ 3300 or 48.4 % of a bank yard, which therefore has a value of $13.98.

This is then the value of the gold in the 10 pound mentioned previously. When the black sands are eliminated you will have gold flakes remaining at the above value. Don't forget the value of the the gold will change with the fluctuating market price of gold. Another way of upping your daily paycheque is to increase your gravel throughput. Remember, the finding of a nugget, a real prize, will materially increase your paycheque (this can happen).

Based on the values given, you can understand why larger mining companies start at 200 yards per day. However by having a two or three person operation we keep the overhead and capital costs at a minimum.

Where do we begin our bulk volume program? We must have easy access to the gravels. If they are bank gravels, no problems here. Stream bed gravels pose problems. We have to bypass the current to get at the gravels. If not too deep, the stream can either be diverted by building a stone dam, called a wing dam, or by diverting the stream through another channel, thus giving access to the bedded gravels.

Keep in mind, do not operate on any creek, river, or pond designated as a salmon hatchery area by the Fisheries Department. A definite no-no.

Once the gravels become available, a transporter is needed. At this economical level it becomes a shovel and wheel barrow operation. As we progress up the economic ladder, transportation converts into a small front end loader and so on up.

We now have our gravels located and a transporter to take them where they will be processed. What now replaces the pan? What recovery system will we use?

The Systems

Many efficient gold recovery systems are available to today's entrepreneur. However several factors must be taken into consideration before deciding on one particular system, chief among them being cost. At this point we balance cost against recovery. For instance size distribution of the gold and system capacity will be strong factors in selecting your recovery system. No use recovering the larger gold flakes which might be only a small percentage of the values while the finer particles are lost in the tailings. Similarly the capacity of the system will have a bearing on recovery. For instance the feed flow rate may be too much thus lowering the efficiency of the gold retrieval system.

Let us start with possibly the simplest system. Next to the pan the gold rocker, one of the earliest systems used, allows the small operator to increase the amount of gravels handled per day as opposed to panning. It is normally a two person operation and will put through 3 - 5 cubic yards in a ten hour shift. If power operated the feed can be increased as high as 2 or 3 yards per hour.See figure 7-2.

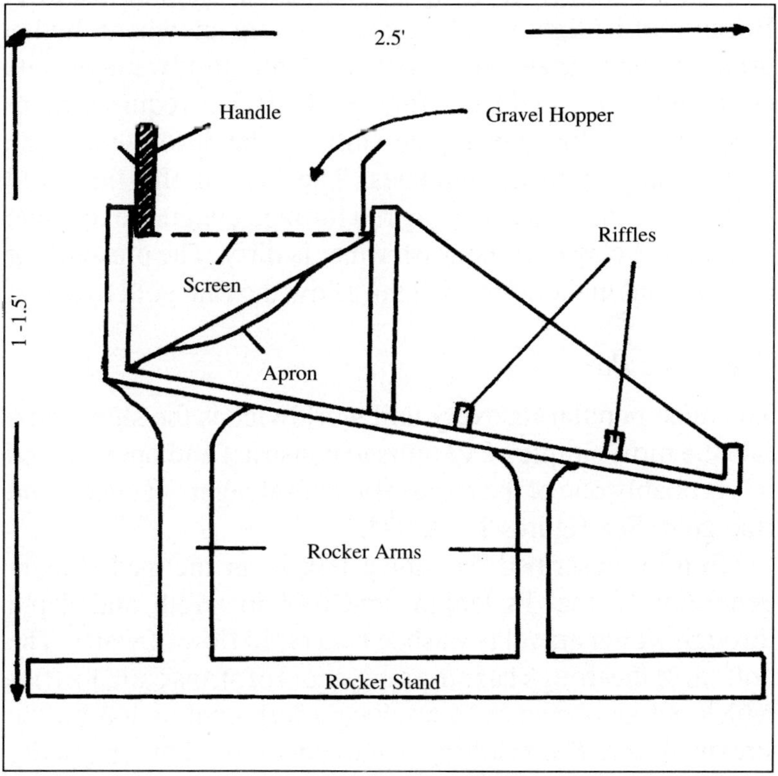

Figure 7-2: Typical Rocker

Material is fed directly to the screen hopper, and then washed by water administered by a ladle or a dipper (larger boulders are screened from the hopper). Additional water is added while the machine is being rocked. The material creeps along the floor of the trough, dependent upon the floor slope, the rocker shake and the quantity of wash water being added. The normal amount of water is generally in the vicinity of 50 to 100 gallons per cubic yard of gravel treated, with the reject water being collected in a waste pond, allowed to settle and then re-used.

The advantage of using a rocker is its manoeuvrability. Because of its light weight it can be set up anywhere. It also uses less water than other systems. A big disadvantage is its poor ability to retain the fine gold. It also requires more frequent cleaning (during the shift) of the apron where the more coarse gold accumulates. The loss of the fine gold increases if the material being run through contains excessive amounts of clay or if the wash water is dirty. The presence of clay or mud in the water will not allow the fine gold to settle.

The Sluice Box

The most popular recovery unit worldwide is the sluice box. It is the most simple of all units to construct and operate, and it is probably one of the more efficient salvagers of coarse and fine gold. See figures 7-3 & 7-4.

Simply described the sluice box is an inclined trough, generally 12 feet in length, one foot in width and depth through which gravel is washed by a rapid flow of water. The bottom of the trough has an arrangement of strips called riffles which act as obstacles to produce a turbulent action on the stream slurry. The resulting phenomenon produces a gravity separation of the heavier minerals alongside the riffles. The heavier particles such as gold and magnetite drop out early and accumulate against the obstruction. This results in a sand bed being produced against the riffles with the larger but lighter particles piling on top.

The resulting topography produces a more turbulent stream action, further agitating the sand bed, which results in more gold deposition and stratification with consequent improved recovery. A "boiling" surface is always a good sign of sluice capability.

Figure 7-3: Single Sluice

The Riffles

The main feature of the sluice box is the riffles. Many studies have been done on different kinds of riffles, and the resulting gold build ups. The most common variety is a strip of wood, iron or steel placed across the width of the sluice box. Often the coarseness of the feed material will dictate the kind of riffle to be used.

The abrasion effect of the fast flowing slurry often rules against using wooden riffles. Types of riffles available (other than those already mentioned) are wooden blocks or poles, stones, iron rails, angle iron, expanded metal and pipe. Their configuration may be either lengthwise or across the box, with the latter most used. The riffles are normally fastened to a rack wedged into the sluice. The wedge makes for easy removal of the riffles for cleaning.

The bed of the sluice box is important. A liner that will collect and hold the fine gold is most desired. Experimentation has run the gauntlet of carpets, screens, burlap, astroturf, and various types of mattings. Most recent tests show for best overall recovery of fine gold, a nomad matting used in conjunction with expanded metal as the sluice riffles recovers approximately 90% of the total gold. The coarse gold or nuggets are best captured using the "Hungarian" or angle iron type of riffle. The term "Hungarian" refers to any type of riffle with an overhang on the downstream side.

Figure 7-4: Multiple Sluices

For the amateur, their 12 foot sluice box should contain 6 - 8 feet of expanded metal riffles overlying nomad matting followed by a 2 foot section of smooth unriffled sluice box, with the final 2 to 4 feet composed of Hungarian riffles over nomad matting to act as a nugget trap.

Sluice Requirements

In the operation of the sluice it was found that the best recovery resulted from a clean water to feed ratio of approximately 4 - 1. For each foot of sluice box width this means that a feed of roughly 400 pounds per minute of solids should be accompanied by some 200 U.S. gallons per minute of fresh water (1 U.S. gallon of water weighs 8.38 pounds). Water can be provided to the sluice box by a hose whose intake end is submerged in the creek at a higher elevation than the sluice box entrance. Or it can be pumped at a greater pressure to the sluice.

The slope of the sluice is very important. Too great a slope means the slurry rushes through the box without an opportunity to settle its content. Too gradual a slope develops a very weak turbulence, hence poor stratification. The usual slope is 1 5/8 inches to 2 inches per foot or 19 1/2 inches to 24 inches from feed to toe of the normal 12 foot sluice. See figure 7-5.

Often the type of gravel feed dictates the slope with flat or shingle type requiring more slope than the rounded type. More slope is also allotted to coarse gravel as opposed to fine. Excessive slope increases sluice wear and decreases riffle effectiveness.

If because of water supply an extreme slope is required to move the heavy slurry, an undercurrent sluice should be provided. This device is a sluice normally 5 to 10 times wider than the main sluice box with a minimum of 10 feet in length. Its main purpose is to salvage the fine gold. Its location is at the end of the main sluice, the tailings from which are fed through a screen with 3/8 inch to 1 inch openings that lead into a launder. This feeds the material evenly across the width of the steeply pitched undercurrent. The undercurrent has matting and riffles similar to the main sluice. It should be understood that if water is sufficient an undercurrent need not be used.

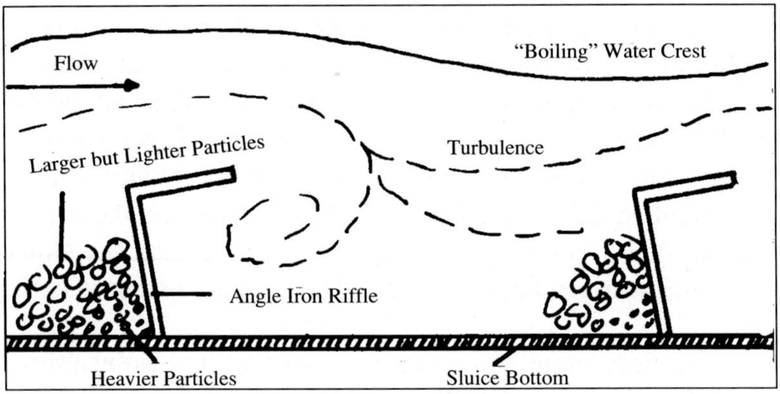

Figure 7-5: Sluice Riffle Action

The Set-Up

It would be advisable to have some form of hopper at the receiving end of the sluice. Feed could be emptied into the hopper and regulated by a choked neck spilling onto a set screen for sizing. See figure 7-6.

In large operations this regulated feed empties into a trommel, a rotating cylindrical screen which sizes the feed according to the screen apertures(See figure 7-7). The larger oversize boulders are thrown out through the open end while the undersize gravel is fed through the openings into a launder, from where it is led by water currents into various sluice boxes.

However in the absence of a feed hopper, the gravel can be fed directly to the head of the sluice by shovelling. It is recommended that a screen be placed at the head of the sluice, with 1/2 inch openings. The gold fines passing through the screen stand a better chance of recovery as proven in tests. The larger portions remaining on the screen can be discarded.

Figure 7-6: Hopper

Sluices are the main tools of the weekend prospectors. They can be manufactured in the basement; can be sectionized; are portable and require little maintenance. In the field they need little supervision; can take large volumes of feed and have a high rate of gold recovery. Usually their concentration ratios are in the extremely high range. Another strong feature — they require a minimal initial investment. On the negative side they are not too effective in recovering very fine gold and do use relatively large amounts of water. In addition they require frequent cleanups.

Figure 7-7: Trommel

Keep in mind the following factors for maintaining good sluice recovery. 1) Don't exceed a feed of 8 cubic yards per hour and 10,000 U.S. gallons of water for the average 12" wide sluice box. 2) Size the feed by means of a screen to allow 1/2" to 3/4" to pass into the sluice box. 3) Use the expanded metal riffles early in the sluice box to collect the finer gold and the Hungarian riffles at the exit end to retrieve the more coarse or nugget type gold. 4) What has been termed a "slick plate section" or sluice with no riffles should be incorporated between the two types of riffles. 5) Use suitable sluice bed underlining for the riffles preferably matting of the cocoa or nomad variety. 6) A slope gradient of 19" to 24" for the average 12 foot sluice box. 7) Appropriate clean-up operations to upgrade concentrates. Don't overpack the riffles!!

For cleanups (gold recoveries), the following procedure is normally followed. The feed gravel is cut off, a large bucket is placed at the overflow end and the sluice rinsed with clear water until the tops of the riffles are clear of gravel. The water is now cut off and the riffles are removed, starting with the one at the head of the sluice. Any obvious coarse gold fragments are removed by hand and deposited in vials. The underlying matting in next removed and both riffle and matting are hosed down with the contents being rinsed into the sluice. Another variation sees the matting being washed and scrubbed in a large wash tub. The operation proceeds section by section down the sluice.

Figure 7-8: Reconcentrating

When all riffles and mats in a sluice have been removed and cleaned, a light flow of water is percolated down the open sluice. The water pressure should be sufficient to move the material slowly. At the same time the concentrate is slowly turned over by means of narrow (4-6 inch) wooden or aluminium shovels which are pushed upstream through the concentrate. This action frees some of the lighter material trapped at the bottom. The concentrate is slowly washed downsluice into the collection bucket(s). During the operation the heavier gold particles will often form a dazzling array of beautiful color grading from coarse through to finer gold at the head of the retreating sluice concentrates. This can be collected or washed into the clean-up bucket.

Upon clean-up completion, the overflow bucket(s) containing the concentrate is emptied and the concentrate further concentrated (to eliminate the black sands) by panning, amalgamating, or running through a clean-up bowl. See figure 7-8.

Mechanical Separators

The above systems are fine and easily operated, however more mechanical systems are coming into play in the last decade or two. These new systems involve centrifugal force in separating the various ingredients of a slurry. The Knelson concentrator is a high speed centrifuge, which when in motion traps the heavier material from the slurry in the ribs of the hopper cone. As water is added during the process the lighter material is slowly perculated out of the wall material and replaced by heavier gold particles of micron and larger sizes. This process tends to enrich the concentrate. Recoveries from these units run as high as 96% of free gold. Knelson have several varieties of concentrators. The smaller 3 inch concentrator handles up to 100 pounds per hour, and lists at approximately $6,300 Canadian. One of its major uses is in the separation of pan or sluice concentrates. Their standard 7 1/2 inch concentrator with screening plant mounted on a prospecting trailer retails for $24,000 Canadian or approximately $20,000 U.S. This unit has a feed capacity of 1/2 cubic yard per hour, and requires

24 U.S. gallons of water per minute. Concentrate stated to be retained is 7 pounds for every cubic yard throughput. The Knelson products are highly regarded within the industry.

One of the earlier concentrators in the centrifugal field is the Knudson bowl. It was designed originally to recover the gold from the concentrate originating from the heavy duty washers. It is confined to feed material primarily in the $^1/_8$ inch and under classification. It will take up to five yards of the screened material per hour and requires 1800 gallons of water to accompany the feed. The removable rubber liner has specially designed undercut riffles, which hold the heavier specific gravity minerals during centrifuging while the lighter material is carried out by the water into the surrounding launder. This established system is operating as a secondary recovery unit at numerous sites. Duke's Mfg. Co. lists it at $3,200. For active work in the field the Knudson bowl requires a screening mechanism in advance to supply the needed mesh size.

Reconcentrating

In addition other companies have available refined concentrators that can be towed or assembled at the desired location. In this category belongs the "Gold Screw", a 180 pound portable that incorporates a hopper with grizzly, a mini trommel and a vibrating gold panner, all driven by a 5 horse power Briggs and Stratton engine. Its capacity is 2 yards per hour and the price tag is $2,800 U.S. It is available from Gold Screw, Inc., Duke's Mfg. Co. and D&K Detector Sales, Inc. in addition to numerous others dealers.

A unit called the "Prospector" with a 2-4 yard per hour capacity is powered through water pressure, supplied by a 5 H.P. centrifugal pump. A hopper feeds a vibrating screen which is lubricated by eight spray nozzles which in addition to scrubbing the feed material also provides sufficient water for the 4 foot by 12 inch underlying sluice box. This recovery system priced at $2,800 U.S. is available from Goldfields Engineering and Machine Works.Figure 7-9.

Let me say there are numerous other wash plants similar in action but varying in design available from many other dealers. I've listed a few to show what is available to the advanced R.V. prospector and to indicate the price ranges. A list of dealers appears in the Appendix. These systems are great when you have plenty of water.

Figure 7-9: Goldfield Prospector

Dry Washers

But how about the dry gulches? Available are several types of dry washers all using a bellows arrangement to supply the air. They can be motorized or hand operated. More modern dry washers incorporate fans hooked up to small portable generator, or plugged into the cigarette outlet of a vehicle. The efficiency of these dry washers is relatively low. Often the concentrates are rerun through the washer or panned. Keene Engineering have introduced a line of mini dry concentrators. One type weighing 21 pounds and suitable for backpacking utilises a pullcord to operate the bellows. An improved version employs the 12 volt battery of a vehicle to drive a cam shaft which in turn vibrates the riffle tray for reportedly improved fine gold recovery. The former sells at $145 while the latter retails at $345.

Some operators who have a modest grade gravel deposit have "imported" their water through a piping system from a nearby reservoir. Others work only during the wet season in order to build temporary reservoirs in which to hold the rain water being washed down the gulches.

Taking the water to the gulch is fine if you have a 1/2 ton truck available. A good number of 45 gallon drums, or large 300 gallon tanks, of water can be placed in the back cargo area and fed to the rocker or sluice box by means of a pump or gravity. I saw an ingenious set up of this nature, where the son of an R.V. owner was hand pumping the water to the small sluice, while his dad shovelled the gravel onto the sluice screen. This water can be recirculated if a proper catching system, such as drums or potholes, is organised at the discharge end. As fine material is washed out along with the water, this material must be allowed to settle prior to re-using the water. These areas for settling are common at active operations where a premium for various reasons (salmon river, low season flow, environmental requirements, etc.) is placed on the water.

There are many ways of working a good placer operations, be it wet or dry, big or little, rich or so-so, so don't be discouraged. The fun comes in improvising. Remember our ancestors did this in the gold rushes of yesteryear. So make your own quiet gold rush, improvise, enjoy the recreational approach and relish the monetary gains provided.

A short summary of some of the more important points of this chapter.

You've decided now that you have your favourite gold claim staked and recorded, you would like to become slightly commercial. Be a little bigger than the amateur. O.K., you have the privilege of concentrating by building and using either a rocker or a sluice box, or purchasing any of the commercial products. In areas of light water supply such as a trickling creek in mid summer or a sidehill gravel-cut some distance from water, the rocker might be just the ticket. If you can motorize it you can put through from 15 to 30 yards per shift. Its efficiency in gold recovery is questionable. If water is no problem, then the sluice box is the answer. Handling more than five times as much feed as the rocker the sluice is efficient, problem free and a joy to use. It is the most recommended gold collection system in use.

Chapter 8

HERE, THERE AND EVERYWHERE

This is a chapter concerning items entirely unrelated to one another. Its a pot pourri of information which I consider you should be aware as a sense of relevance. The only common thread is placer mining.

Assessment

The Federal government in all its graciousness requires that we do work on our located claims on an annual basis. Although we have staked and laid claim to the ground, it is ours only on right of possession and "lease", to speak, from the Federal Government. They want some activity, money-wise, done on the property. It is ours only after we have had a legal survey conducted on the claim. It then becomes fee land for which taxes are paid

The rules for assessment work, in any state in the Union, require that $100 worth of work be performed on each claim annually, followed by the paperwork and filing. $100 a claim is really not bad! The work is supposedly directed towards proving that mineralization exists on the claim and that a reasonable prospect of success will exist in marketing the product. The buzz words are 'exist' and 'reasonable'.

With placering, as I stated earlier, you proved the existence of gold when it appeared in your pan. No worry about "mineralization existing". As to the marketability — there is a ready market for the product. The economical factors come into play as the operation enlarges. A family operation making a holiday of the adventure will turn a profit no matter what price you put on the wife and kids labor. It's when expansion includes capital purchase of big machinery and outside labor costs that the profit angle becomes more of a concern.

What is acceptable for assessment work? Obviously mining is the best form whether it be panning, sluicing or rockering. This is work being done on the claim. So, put a price — reasonable — on your hourly stint. If you claim $5 an hour as your wages, obviously in two 10 hour shifts you will have filled the $100 assessment requirement for that claim.

Next in line to actual mining, is excavation work. If you are working a high bank with a pay zone under a good amount of non-paying gravels you may want to run a drift, a horizontal tunnel, at the elevation of the pay zone thus eliminating all the overlying waste work. Or if you are in a dry gulch with evidence that gold values lie some distance below the poorly mineralized upper section, you may wish to "sink shafts" — vertical excavations — to the desired horizon. These workings (excavations) may need shoring — timbering — to keep the gravels from caving or they could conversely "stand up" without the timber.

Another type of work is road building. Your claim might be isolated and require some form of trail or route to it. And then there is sampling and assaying. These include the cost of physically taking the sample and the laboratory's charge for analysing it. And finally there is a geological or geophysical survey. These latter surveys require a technical report to accompany the affidavit of work.

Upon completion of the assessment work, an affidavit is drawn up listing the charges and type of work on the claim. It need not be attested to. A requirement is that this assessment work be completed on the claim by September 1st of each year and then be recorded in both the County recorder's office and the Bureau of Land Management office by specified dates. In all the states, the recording date for the B.L.M is December 31st of that year. At the county court house it varies according to the state. With:

California - affidavit must be recorded within 30 days of completing the work or October 1st of that year.
Nevada - the final recording date is November 1st of that year.
Arizona - the recording date is similar to the B.L.M., that is December 31st of that year.

Do keep your assessment up. It's an awful surprise to find that the claims came open due to lack of recording the assessment work and somebody else staked the ground.

To bring your claims to fee simple — that is privately owned or patented ground — you will require a Mineral Patent Survey. This brings into play a special group of mineral surveyors who are acquainted with the requirements. They will do the perimeter and required surveying and submit the work to yourself and the B.L.M. Following the submission you will be informed by the B.L.M. of the result and the taxes that will be levied against the property. I do not recommend this approach due to the high cost of the survey. It may be just the ticket however if your visits are sporadic and might give rise to losing the claims.

Figure 8-1: Dredge

Amalgamation

In Chapter 6 I briefly reported on this process. It is a method of retrieving the fine gold that lingers in a gold pan. It is also a fast way of capturing the gold contained in the concentrate as opposed to running through the complete panning procedure and possibly losing some fine gold to the overflow.

One item, mentioned previously must be emphasized again. Oil which contains a fatty acid or a fatty-acid salt is a bad contaminator. Most oils fall into this category. Ensure that your pan, rocker, and sluice is in no way subject to this contamination.

The concentrate from the panning, rockering or sluicing operations following drying and magnetic extraction may still contain some heavy, light colored minerals in addition to the gold particles. The nugget size gold pieces have by now been carefully picked out and set apart leaving the finer gold to be subjected to amalgamation. Don't forget that the metal for amalgamation needs to be a clean, bright gold. If it is tarnished or dirty its amalgamation properties are somewhat limited. Normally placer gold is a clean type as it has been derived from primary quartz veins.But if sulphides, particularly bismuth and antimony in the oxide form are present, the amalgamation process is weakened. However don't lose any sleep over these factors. The odds are greatly in your favor of having a placer with clean native gold.

The separation of the mercury from the gold amalgam by the use of heat — that is distilling the mercury into a gaseous form and then condensing back to the liquid state — is known as retorting. The residue which is left in the pot following this procedure is a gold sludge with a few minor impurities. The tremendous difference in the boiling points of mercury (675° F) and gold (4,720° F) is the factor in this separation.

A mercury retort apparatus is generally of a three unit type, each unit serving a different function. The iron pot is the initial holder of the amalgam and the final recipient of the gold residue. These jars are available in all sizes. I would suggest a medium sized one with a capacity of 2 to 3 pounds. The jar can be heated in a variety of ways but the handiest and probably the best is the blow torch. Normally this is not supplied with the complete apparatus but can be purchased at a K-Mart or automotive outlet store. Remember to start with low heat, gradually increasing it. Also to avoid any choking at the jar outlet, do not fill the jar beyond the half full mark with amalgam. See figure 6-2.

The condenser section consists of a glass or metal sleeve outletting from the jar and some four to six feet in length. Its function is to conduct the gaseous mercury fumes from the jar down through the lengthy sleeve to an outlet just below water level in an open glass container. The condenser has an outer section, a water jacket so to speak, through which cold water is continually running. The drop in temperature as the mercury gas travels the sleeve gradually condenses it to its liquid form. Early placer prospectors wrapped potato sacking or a coarse cloth around the lengthy inner pipe and kept pouring water from a bucket over the sacking. There is no reason why this procedure can not be adopted today, if it should become necessary.

The outlet end of the condenser is located just below the the water surface of a catching bowl.Its location here is to ensure that any fumes which escape from the condenser will condensate in the water-filled bowl and also to act as a safety feature. Upon completion of the operation gradually lower the heat under the amalgam jar until the jar is cool.Should the heat be suddenly withdrawn from under the jar it will create a vacuum which will suck the water from the bowl through the condensor into the hot jar and possibly cause an explosion. Therefore ensure that the discharge end is just slightly *below* the water level of the bowl as the heat is being lowered.

It is again emphasized that mercury fumes are poisonous and all exit points from the jar should be well sealed to avoid escape. In addition the whole operation should be conducted in the open air. Avoid close spaces.The mercury that appears in the bottom of the collecting bowl may be used for further amalgamation.

Small retort units if purchased at mining suppliers run in the $60 range without the addition of liquid mercury ($50 - $60 per 2 lb. jar) or a heating unit, such as a blow torch ($15 - $25).

Other Forms of Placer Mining

Dredging:

This highly commercialized form of placer mining involves a combination of an elevating excavator, a concentrating plant and a tailings disposal unit, all contained within a flat, shallow barge. Like a barge they utilize natural bodies of water or they develop their own ponds from their advance excavating coupled with overflow water. Their excavating arm consists of a series of buckets on a continuous line which extract gravel from 35 - 50 feet below the pond level. Their target is normally the fine gold distributed in wide deltaic valleys, flood plains or relatively shallow lake bottoms. See figure 8-1.

The foregoing data on dredges is just for general information. Dredging was particularly popular at the turn of the century and during the 1930's depression. An offshoot of that for the weekend prospector or active RV entrepreneur is scuba dredging (skin diving). I personally have not done anything of this nature, primarily because I'm a poor swimmer. If you become involved, be very safety conscious with regards to tides, currents, navigational hazards and the limitations of the dredge you are working with.This is popular in certain areas of the Sierra Nevadas of California.

Scuba Dredging:

This refers to any sub-surface aquatic search for gravels or gold bearing sands. The action might involve river bed gravels only a few feet below the surface or it might refer to deeper lake or river bottoms. The miner could be knee deep in water,snorkelling at a shallow depth or even using compressed air lines, at a moderate depth.

The suction dredges are built for portability (45-60 lbs. for back packing; and up to 400 lbs. for truck transportation) and are classified according to the diameter of the suction tube. In general, the unit consists of a gas engine coupled to a water pump, a 36" to 60" sluice(s) and variable lengths of suction hose. For back packing purposes, the unit is mounted on a light weight frame and may be supplied with an inflatable truck tube or pontoons for flotation. The larger units are welded together and attached to modular heavy duty pontoons. The dredges start at the 2" hose size and graduate through 2 1/2", 3" and 4" to the 5" present maximum. All save the smallest have the capability of adding a compressor to the flotation unit to supply air for divers. The dredging depth varies from a few feet to 25 feet as a safe depth. The capacity of the sluice(s) increases with the size of the unit with a maximum of 16 yards per hour being reached at the 5" size. Prices start at $750 for the 2" back packs and pass the $2750 mark for the larger sizes. The smaller models are also portable enough for mining the high bank gravels while their pump (detached) at the water's edge carries water up to the operating point. See figure 8-2.

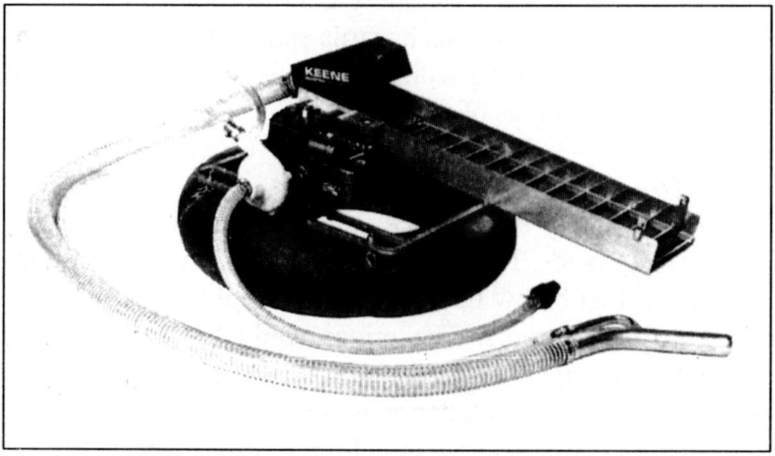

Figure 8-2: Scuba Dredge (Keene)

Shaft Sinking and Drift Mining:
Earlier in this chapter I referred to this type of mining as an assessment counter. It also is a means of exploration, a favorite approach of the old-time placer prospector.

If the overburden is relatively thick over the gravels or if the upper portion of the gravels is unproductive, the prospector of yesteryear would often sink a prospect shaft through the weak valued material until he reached the gold bearing gravels. These shafts vary from openings 5 feet by 5 feet down to 2 feet by 3 feet. Oftentimes if the overburden or the gravels "run", that is have a tendency to cave in, the shaft is timbered. If the depth is not too great and the gravels hold up the prospector might take a chance on going down without timbering.The shallow shafts, up to 10 to 15 feet deep, have been used to outline paystreaks along old river course

Several decades ago while examining a placer property in the Yukon Territory, my prospector friend and myself trudged several miles up a tributary creek checking the gravels as we progressed. Over the 2 mile distance I counted close to 60 shallow shafts that had been put down in the bank alongside this particular creek by miners in the 1896-98 Klondike rush. Obviously these miner-prospectors were trying to outline a pay streak that had developed in the ancient creek bed many eons before. Over the intervening 75 years the majority of the shafts had caved in but a few appeared to be open. I was not adventurous enough to try to descend to the bottom. In the Yukon — as with Alaska and certain northern areas of British Columbia — the permafrost (permanently frozen ground) can extend down to 100 feet. This frozen ground is excellent to shaft through as little, if any, timbering is required. In summer the sun might melt an area of the shaft close to the surface so that often this initial 6 to 8 feet is timbered to prevent the thawed material from sloughing in.

In some cases when these shafts meet the rocky bottom of the old stream the veteran placer miner will drift along the pay streak, that is he will excavate a horizontal tunnel on the rock floor. If this is to be the case the shaft then becomes a little more elaborate in design and size, as he must haul the gravels to the shaft and there hoist them to the surface, allow them to thaw, then run them through his sluiceboxes.

One placer property in northern British Columbia was into a commercial operation on claims that had been noted for years as carrying good gold values. The claims were located on the old Tertiary channel. The present day stream had been rerouted probably by the last ice age (Wisconsin) plus later uplifting and erosion. The latter process had likely been the more influential in this relocation and had moved the present day stream some 600 yards to the west. The old channel bed lay 135 feet below the surface. The present operators had removed some 30 feet of overburden and were now systematically open-pitting the great thickness of gravels. They were putting some 400-600 yards of gravel through their 3 sluice boxes each 10 hour shift. There were three pay zones in the 135 foot thickness. Obviously the creek had dry periods at which time the fine clay in suspension was deposited where it dried and formed a false bottom. When the stream ran again the gravels were deposited on this clay bed. However the amazing thing about this deposit were the myriad of tunnels, many timbered, that were uncovered during the pit excavation. These tunnels were run at the interface of the bouldery gravels with the underlying rock. As witnessed by the values emerging from the sluices this six to ten foot thickness — from bedrock up — was the best pay zone for gold values. These drifts, run off inclined shafts, had been located by placer miners in the 1910-1925 era. They had drifted along the most promising pay streaks. Modern technology caught up to them a half century later.

Jigs

The action of a jig is very similar to that of the pan or the sluice — classification by gravity concentration. However where the pan and rocker form their beds by shaking and the sluice by means of the stirring action of eddying water impulses, the jig effects separation by the pulsating action of the feed material acting on the beds. Remember they all form beds. The pan action washes away the lighter material leaving the black sand concentrate; a similar result occurs behind the riffles of the sluice. In the jig the feed (gravel and water) enters, collects on a screen and is continually subjected to an

Figure 8-3: Jig

up and down pulsating action. This pulsating action sorts the grains of the feed into layers according to their weight and size. Again as with the pan and sluice the heavier materials fight their way to the bottom (in the jig case — the screen) while the lighter material rises to the top of the bed where they are whisked away into the overflow. The heavier screen size particles (fine concentrate) pass through the screen into a lower compartment known as a hutch. Those particles of a similar specific gravity but unfortunately of a bigger size than the screen openings, form the bottom portion of the jig bed (coarse concentrate).

Jigs often consist of multiple cells with the hutch of each cell yielding succeeding lower grade concentrates. Many times these jigs are entered into a circuit very early (often prior to the trommel) where their prime concern is capturing nuggets. For this they are given the term "scalpers". Jigs can vary in size from the small single unit of 8 by 12 inch often used in conjunction with sluices to the larger 24 by 36 inch multiple cell size as used in milling circuits. (See figure 8-3).

For the RV gold seeker jigs are something to be understood but need not be used in his operations. They are one more method employed to trap gold.

Disposal Sites:

This has no significance unless you have graduated from the pan or rocker into the larger category of sluice box operations. And even here it has little consequence unless your throughput on a daily average exceeds 20 to 30 yards. This means you are wheelbarrowing in excess of 110 to 160 loads of gravel to the sluice daily or on a 10 hour shift one every 5 minutes. Some hustling!! However setting up at the creek edge overcomes most of this haulage.

Seriously, if you are still a small operation, set up by the creek edge and drawing your feed by means of shovels from a nearby bank, you are running a lot of water and gravel out of the lower end of your sluice as tailings. Eventually the water will create a pond and the waste gravel will start to fill it. In production language this becomes known as a disposal site. (See figure 8-4). You are disposing of muddy water and piling all the waste gravel in a specific location.In the old days the sluice box operator would run his overflow — water and

Figure 8-4: Tailings Disposal

tailings — back into the creek. However in these environmentally-conscious days we are more careful. At a big operation, the storage of this waste water and overflow material becomes quite a problem. These facilities provide what are termed "settling ponds" for the overflow water. These ponds are dug relatively deep and the overflow is directed to them be means of pipes or hoses. There can be anywhere up to 3 or 4 of these settling ponds on an active property. They are routinely rotated so as to allow the suspended material to settle to the bottom. The clear water meanwhile is allowed to percolate through to the water table or is evaporated by the sun or reused One enterprising company pumped this water up to a sprinkling system located high in trees. This system was given the OK by the US Forestry Department as the aerated water was considered similar to rain for the surrounding vegetation. Seldom is permission given nowdays to pump the water directly back into the river or creek. When a pond fills with gravel it is cleared by a front end loader.

Figure 8-5: Oversize Disposal

Another area that must be considered by an advanced operator is a waste disposal site. At this site is disposed all the oversize rocks, pebbles, etc. which were spilled out of the trommel. These collected at the open exit of the latter and generally consist of rocks is excess of 2" in diameter. See figure 8-5. A collection pit is normally dug at this open end and when deemed necessary a front end loader hauls this rock wastage away and stacks it at the waste disposal site. It is surprising to see the difference in rock sizes in these disposal areas. In Alaska for instance, where glaciation has been more effective, the sites contain huge boulders often up to several feet in width. This contrasts with the smaller pebble sites of the southwest.

Economics

We discussed this briefly in Chapter 7 but let's have a more definitive look at it.

In placering we are trying to free gold from entrapment in certain substances, normally a gold-bearing gravel. The S.G. (specific gravity) of the average gold gravel is 125 pounds per cubic foot (16 cubic feet = 1 ton). The S.G. of clean sand averages 100 pounds per cubic foot (20 cubic feet = 1 ton). As an aside, and this is where my background comes in, the average S.G. for rock taken from an underground(or surface) mining operation is 170 pounds to the cubic foot (12 cubic feet = 1 ton) depending upon the percentage of sulphide minerals within the rock. This can go as high as 200-220 pounds to the cubic foot.

Remember that a ton of rock weighs 2000 pounds while a yard of gold-gravel weighs 3300 pounds (125 lbs. times 27 cubic feet). This volume (yard) to weight (pound) measurement causes problems. Many times we have to transpose one to the other. For example:

How many yards (y) in 200 tons?

200 tons = y yards

200 x 2000 = y x 3300

$\frac{200 \times 2000}{3300}$ = y yards

121.21 yards (y) = 200 tons

Verification:

200 tons x 2000 pounds = 121.21 yards x 330pounds

400, 000 = 399, 993

Now the assay comes in from the analyst and it is normally expressed in ounces gold per ton. We know that a yard of gravel weights more than a ton of rock. So presuming the gold is evenly distributed, there will be more ounces of gold in 3300 pounds (yard) than in 2000 pounds (ton). The conversion factor will be 1.65 in going from ounces per ton to ounces per yard or 0.61 if going in the reverse direction. For example:

How many ounces of gold in a yard (z) when assay is 0.05 ounces gold per ton (or 0.05 per 2000 pounds)?

$$\frac{0.05}{2000} = \frac{z}{3300}$$

$$0.05 \times 3300 = z \times 2000$$

=0.0825 ounces gold per yard.

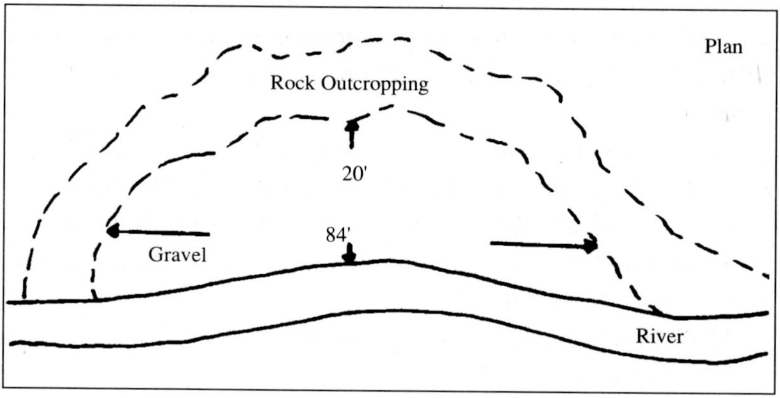

Figure 8-6: Gravel Estimation

Many times you must go from volume to weight to determine tonnage and conversely from assay results expressed in tons to find the overall amount of gold in a defined block of gravel. For example:

In a bank gravel deposit alongside a creek we measure the dimensions and find the width from rivers edge to rock outcropping to be 20 feet. We are also hemmed in on the length , or longitudinal measurement, by further rock outcrops but our measurement is 84 feet. We have put a pit down to bedrock in the middle of our gravel exposure. It went down 6 feet. See Figure 8-6.

On the presumption that the river eroded the rock evenly and that the rocky stream bed is the same rock that outcrops on the shoreline, we have a gravel volume within this area of:

20 foot width x 84 foot length x 6 foot depth
= 10,080 cubic feet (ft^3)
or = 373 cubic yards (yd^3)
or = 616 tons gravel.

If a sample of the auriferous gravel is sent to a laboratory for an analysis and is returned to us as 0.035 ounces gold per ton, then the 616 tons of gravel contains

616 x 0.035 = 21.55 ounces of gold
scattered within the gravel deposit.
(approximately $7500 at the present $350 gold price)

That assay upon conversion to ounces gold per yard becomes 0.0578. Expressing it in the volume contents it becomes 373 x 0.0578 = 21.55 ounces of gold in the deposit.

Reworked Ground

As an aside note some of the surface forms in previously worked areas such as ravines or deltaic valleys. Many times they have a hummocky or very rough surface outline which is due to the distribution of the placer rejects from the previous operators of the area.Over the years vegetation has overgrown the rejects leaving the surface in this condition. Do remember that no matter how many times an area has been worked by placer operators each working, or reworking, is an indication that there are, or were, traces of gold values in that section. Please be aware that, as a rule, not all gold is recovered in most mining (or placering) operations. So there is still room to GO FOR THE GOLD!

APPENDIX

Conversion Tables

Weight (Troy)

1 pound = 12 ounces = 5760 grains
1 ounce = 480 grains = 31.103 grams = 20 pennyweight
1 gram = 15.433 grains.

Liquid Volume

1 US gallon = 0.833 British gallons = 3.785 litres
1 U.S. gallon = 0.134 cubic feet = 8.38 pounds

Measurement (Linear)

1 foot =12 inches = 30.48 centimeters = 0.305 meters.
1 meter = 39.370 inches =100 centimeters =1000 millimeters.
1 inch = 2.54 centimeters = 25.4 millimeters.
1 centimeter = 0.394 inches =10 millimeters.

Measurement (Surveyed Area)

1 township = 36 square miles = 23040 acres
1 section =1 square mile = 640 acres = 259 hectares
1 acre = 0.405 hectares = 43,560 square feet

Approximate Weights per cubic foot

Solid Rock =170 pounds per cubic foot (12 cubic feet = 1 ton)
Gold Gravels = 125 pounds per cubic foot (16 cubic feet = 1 ton.)
Clean Sands = 100 pounds per cubic foot (20 cubic feet = 1 ton.)

Weight to Volume Conversion Factor (Placer)

1.65 tons = 1 bank yard = 1.4 loose yards
1.00 ton = 0.67 bank yard = 0.93 loose yard

Gold Sizes

Coarse Gold= larger than 10 mesh
Medium Gold= 10 to 20 mesh
Fine Gold= 20 to 40 mesh
Flour Gold (Colors)= finer than 40 mesh

Mesh Size (Diameter of Opening Size)

MESH	*MILLIMETERS*	*INCHES*
4	4.28	.1685
8	2.045	.0805
10	1.70	.0609
12	1.56	.0530
14	1.40	.0444
20	0.850	.0331
28	0.680	.0268
32	0.595	.0234
40	0.425	.0167
48	0.297	.0117
65	0.200	.0079
100	0.149	.0059
150	0.105	.0041

Transporting Power of Water
(Fom Mining Engineers Hand Book)

Velocity in		*Material*
Ft/sec.	*MPH*	*Moved*
15	(10)	Begins to wear away fine clay
30	(20)	Just lifts fine sand
60	(41)	Moves fine gravel
180	(123)	Moves pebbles of egg size
300	(205)	Moves stones 3-4 inches in diameter
400	(273)	Moves stones 6-8 inches in diameter

Karat System

24 Karat =	100%	gold (pure gold)
18 Karat =	75%	gold
14 Karat =	58.3%	gold
10 Karat =	41.7%	gold
8 Karat =	33.3%	gold

THE GEOLOGICAL TIME SCALE

(Time shown in Millions of Years)

ERA	PERIOD	DATES	MISC.
Quaternary	Recent	0 - 01	
	Pleistocene	01 - 2	Stone (Ice)Age
Tertiary	Pliocene	2 - 7	Man Appears
	Miocene	7 - 26	Mammals Reach Climax
	Ol igocene	26 - 38	Apes Appear
	Eocene	38 - 54	Modern Order Appears
	Paleocene	54 - 65	Old Mammals Dominate
Mesozoic	Cretaceous	65- 135	Dinosaurs At Peak
	Jurassic	135 - 195	Toothed Birds Appear
	Triassic	195 - 225	Small Mammals Appear
Paleozoic	Permian	225 - 280	Mountain Making
	Carbonaceous	280 - 345	Coal Making
	Devonian	345 - 395	Forests Appear
	Silurian	395-435	CoralReefs
	Ordovician	435-500	Seas Inundate Lands
	Cambrian	500 - 600	Low Marine Life
PRE-CAMBRIAN		600 - 4500	No Known Life

The Recleaning of Concentrates

The concentrates derived from a days panning,or the clean-up of a sluice run, are treated further to eliminate the impurities. This can be done by putting them through a bowl concentrator (such as the Goldhound) or a shaker table (such as the Wilfley). There is more room in an RV for a bowl concentrator as opposed to a shaker table.

Prior to the recleaning it would be adviseable to dry the concentrates and then put them through a Tyler 20 and a 40 mesh screen.From this will result three size fractions: that is (1) greater than 20 mesh, contains the coarse and medium gold fragments, (that left on the 20 mesh screen), (2) from -20 to +40 , contains the fine gold (that fraction that passes through the 20 mesh screen but remains on the 40 mesh screen) and finally (3) the undersize contains the flour gold, that which passes through the 40 mesh size.

The reason for sizing at this point is to allow yourself an idea from which fraction the greater amount of gold is derived. This affords some considerations should changes in the sluice design be contemplated.

The sized samples are treated separately in the bowl concentrator, It is a good practice to treat each sample twice over. The first cleaning utilizes the full-sized fraction while the second cleaning involves the recovered concentrate which carries all the gold and some of the black sands., Following the second pass, the concentrate is almost pure gold with but a few impurities. During these runs a liquid dishwashing detergent may be used as a wetting agent to reduce the surface tension of the water used. In particular this acts on the flour gold reducing its tendency to float off with the tailings.

Don't forget when running the different size fractions through the bowl to adjust the bowl angle to obtain the best separation. The instruction booklet with the concentrator will specify optimum angles. Following the last concentration, the concentrated sample should have whatever magnetic particles remain removed by a magnet. If further impurities remain try a little bit of careful panning in a bucket.

This finally leaves you with the sized recovered gold. If you wish to size more thoroughly, you can, otherwise the gold is ready for sale. A short list of refineries follows in subsequent pages.

REFINING

What the refinery does is melt your concentrate down until a separation of the precious metals from the impurities is effected.You can use the refinery for several different purpose:

(1) They will buy your gold.
(2) They will refine the concentrate and place the gold metal in a pool account.
(3) They will return the dollar equivalent to you as a fabricated material or in the form of bullion,coin or wafers (Eagles, MapleLeafs etc)

There are numerous refineries of which I list a few later in this Appendix. The charges vary but are, in general,very similar.

You are charged for the assay of the material you send in. This gives the refinery an idea what to expect from your shipment.

In the refining you will receive credit for a percentage of each precious metal recovered. This varies from 95% to 98.5% of the total metal.The percentage you do not receive belongs to the refinery. In addition you will be charged a sum for each ounce extracted. Some refineries make a minimum deduction of ounces gold from the recovered amount (this is their servicing charge) then pay you for a percentage (in the mid 90%) of the remaining amount.Price settlement is made in several ways,one being the second or final London daily gold fix, or it may be based on Metals Week average, or Handy & Harmon daily fix. It might be well to request a refining charge schedule from the refinery before making a shipment.

As an example, let's assume you ship 100 pounds of a retorted spongy mass or a similar amount of black sands sluice concentrate to a refinery:

The refineries assay shows:
245.3 ounces gold per ton.
75.0 ounces silver per ton.
(You pay $25 for this assay)
In the refining:
100 pounds (1/20 of a ton) yields
= 12.265 ounces gold
= 3.75 ounces silver

Settlement (say): Gold (London) $350/ounce
Silver (New York) $ 4/ounce
Refinery Charges : $ 8.00/ oz.Gold
$ 0.75/ oz.Silver

Therefore:

You pay : 12.265 @ $8.00 per ounce gold
= $98.12
3.75 @ $0.75 per ounce silver
= 2.81
(Refinery Charges) $100.93

You receive : (12.265 @ $350) x 98% gold
= $4206.90
(3.75 @ $ 4) x 95% silver
= 14.25
(From Sales) $4221.15

Your recovery is	=	$ 4221.15
less refinery	=	- 100.93
less assaying	=	- 25.00
Total		$ 4095.22

Not all refineries will pay for the included platinum or palladium if such is present. If you request an assay for these precious metals and payment for presence you might add slightly more to your take home pay. Just suppose there was one quarter of an ounce of platinum and palladium present although you might pay more for the refining, you do end up on the plus side.

An assay for these two metals might be the same as silver-gold ,that is $25.

The refining charges are normally much higher (say $25 per ounce) and the percentage credited slightly lower (say 95%). Even though the final recovery is below an ounce you will still be charged the full ounce price. You are now paying the refinery $ 75 for the assaying and the refinery price of the two metals. But wait, look at the present sales price of these two precious metals - platinum $355 per ounce while palladium hovers near the $90 mark. So you receive a gross of $105.69 less charges of $75 for a net of $30.69. Enough to buy baby a new pair of shoes!!

MINING SUPPLY DEALERS

The following list contains but a fraction of the prospecting supply houses throughout the nation. In the interests of brevity I have selected only a few. However the omission of a dealer's name, in no way implies they are not reliable. I suggest you check the Yellow Pages under Mining-Supplies for local dealers.

The Prospectors Cache,
3461 South Broadway,
Englewood, CO 80110
(303) 781-8787

D & K Detector Sales,
13809 S.E. Division St.,
Portland, OR 97236
(503) 761-1521

Duke's Mfg. Co.,
2500 - Z Valley Road,
Reno, NV 89512
(702) 322-1629

Goldfields Engineering &
Machine Works,
P.O. Box 177,
Provo, UT 84603 (801) 374-6611

Prescott Gold Prospectors,
201 North Cortez,
Prescott, AZ 86301

The Prospector,
905 E. Broadway
Glendale, CA 91205

Keene Engineering Inc.,
9330 Corbin Ave.,
Northridge, CA 91324
(818) 993-0411

Darwin's Treasure Finders,
4478 Park Blvd.,
Pinellas Park, FL 33565

Knelson International Sales Inc.,
20313 86th Ave.,
Langley, B.C. Canada V3A 6Y3
(604) 888-4000

REFINERIES

The following list contains the names and addresses of several refineries within the United States. The omission of other refineries in no way implies any apprehension as the list has been shortened for brevity sake.

David H. Fell & Co. Inc.
4176 Pacific Way,
Los Angeles, CA 90023

Johnson Matthey Inc.
4601 W. 2100 S,
Salt Lake City, UT 84120

Rocky Mountain Refining,
6111 Menaul Blvd. NE,
Albuquerque, NM 87710

William Advanced Materials,
c/o Brush Wellman Inc.,
2978 Main Street,
Buffalo, NY 14214

Englehard Industries West Inc.,
5510 E. La Palma Ave.,
Anaheim, CA 92807

HARDNESS-SPECIFIC GRAVITY LIST

Mineral	Primary Metal	Specific Gravity	Hardness
Apatite	Phosphate	3.2	5
Argentite	Ag	7.3	2-2.5
Arsenopyrite	As	6.1	5.5-6
Barite	Ba	4.5	3-3.5
Beryl	Beryllium	2.8	7.5-8
Calcite	Ca	2.7	3
Cassiderite	Sb	7.0	6-7
Chalcopyrite	Cu	4.2	3.5-4
Corundum	Al	4.0	9
Diamond	C	3.5	10
Fluorite	F	3.2	4
Galena	Pb	7.5	2.5
Garnet	Silicate	3.9	6.5-7.5
Gold	Gold	19.3	2.5-3
Gypsum	Ca	2.3	2
Magnetite	Fe	5.2	6
Molybdenite	Mo	4.7	1-1.5
Opal	Silicate	2.1	5-6
Orthoclase	Mixture	2.6	6
Platinum	Pl	16.0	4-4.5
Pyrite	Fe	5.0	6-6.5
Pyrrhotite	Fe	4.6	4
Quartz	Silicate	2.7	7
Silver	Ag	10.5	2.5-3
Sphalerite	Zn	4.0	3.5-4
Talc	Mg	2.7	1
Tourmaline	Boron	3.2	7-7.5
Zircon	Zirconium	4.7	7.5

Hardness Scale

1 - 2.5 = Can be scratched by fingernail.
2.5 - 3 = Can be scratched by a penny.
3 - 5.5 = Can be scratched by a knife.
5.5 - 7 = Can be scratched by quartz.
7 - 10 = Cannot be scratched by quartz.

NOTICE OF LOCATION
(Placer Mining Claim)

The undersigned, having complied with the requirements of Title 30, United States Code, Section 35, and the local laws, customs and regulations of this State, did on ____________________ locate this the ______________________________ PLACER MINING CLAIM upon a valuable placer mineral deposit containing ______________ and other locatable minerals situated in the ______________ Mining District, ______________ County, State of ____________ .

[If claim boundaries do not conform exactly with legal subdivisions of surveyed section, here insert proper courses and distances for each segment of claim boundaries.]

This claim comprises the ______________________________ of Section __________, Township _________, Range __________, of the _________ Base and Meridian, and contains _________ acres.

The Discovery Monument upon which a copy of this Notice is conspicuously posted is situated ____________________ a distance of __________ feet from the _________ corner of this claim. Nearby local landmarks are: ____ .

Name of Locator(s): ____

Address: ____

____

GLOSSARY

A.S.L. Above sea level.
Ag Chemical symbol for silver.
Alluvial Fan River discharge of gravel as it emerges from canyons and gulches.
Alluvial Detrital material transported by water and deposited at points.
Amalgam Mixture of gold and mercury.
Argentiferous Containing silver.
Arroyo Dry stream bed.
Assay To evaluate the amount and type of metals in an ore sample
Assessment Work required by B.L.M. on a located claim.
Au Chemical symbol for gold.
Auriferous Containing gold.

B.L.M. Federal organization called Bureau of Land Management.
Bajada placer A deposit of alluvial and eluvial material formed along the base of mountain ranges in arid regions (sometimes called desert placer).
Bar A shallow sand and/or gravel deposit normally across rivers. Generally associated with gold.
Bed Rock Unweathered rock below soil cover.

Bench A gravel terrace above the present river bank left by an ancient river.

Black sands Concentration of heavy dark minerals following panning. May contain gold.

Caliche Hard layer of calcium carbonate-cemented gravels, usually at or near surface.

Cemented gravel Gravels bound together by a cementing agency such as iron or lime to form a hard layer.

Chalcopyrite An ore of copper. Coupled with iron and sulphur.

Circuit Sequence of mechanical and chemical operations applied to removing metals from minerals and rocks.

Claim That portion of mining ground held under the Federal and local laws by one claimant,or association,by virtue of location and record. Often called a location.

Clay Generally very fine particles which form a plastic bed when wet while becoming impervious when dry to form a bedding layer.

Col Depression or canyon in mountain.

Color Gold flakes finer than 40 mesh (0.017 inches or .43 millimeters) Often called flour gold.

Concentrate grade Is the percentage of gold in the concentrate.

Concentrate Mixture of heavy black sands and heavier pieces of ore which carry gold.

Conglomerate In geology,it is a sedimentary rock consisting of a mixture of very fine to fine fragments plus larger well-rounded pebbles.

Contiguous Touching. Normally refers to claims which adjoin to one another.

Density Is the weight per unit volume of a substance.

Deposit An accumulation of material in one location.
Detritus Material produced following erosional effects.
Dip The slope of an angle with reference to the horizontal.
Dredging A method of collecting ,or vacuuming, gold-bearing gravels from a river or lake bottom.
Drift A horizontal passage underground which follows a vein or mineralized structure.
Dry Washer A mechanical device that separates gold from gravels by the flow of forced air.

Eluvial Placer deposits formed without stream action, upon hill slopes due to erosion.
Erosion The breakdown of rock masses due to the effects of weathering.

False Bedrock Often a hard clay bed mistaken for consolidated rocks.
Fee Land Private land upon which taxes are paid. Do not encroach upon without owner's permission.
Feed Flow Amount of gravel fed to the front end of a concentrating unit.
Float Rock portions of an eluvial placer away from its point of origin.
Fool's Gold Name given to iron pyrite which is often mistaken visually for gold.

Galena An ore of lead. Coupled with sulphur.
Gangue The weak valued minerals that are present in the vein or ore deposit in addition to the economic minerals.
Glacial Debris The unassorted material that drops out of a glacier as it retreats.
Gravel The fine rock particles that accumulate following erosion and weathering.

Grizzly A heavy iron grid used at the feed end to size the material. Generally eliminates large boulders.
Gumbo A very silty clay usually sticky when wet and hard when dry. Found in the southern states.

Hard Pan Refers to iron cemented clay and gravel layers normally found at the base of soils.
High Grade Usually refers to a high assay value placed on the precious metals.

Intrusive A deepseated emplacement of a rock type (usually granite or granodiorite) into a previously consolidated strata.

Launder A collecting box (such as on a trommel) which evenly distributes the collected material to other agencies (such as sluice boxes)
Limit The outside edges of a channel.
Lithify The consolidation of sediments into rock formations(such as gravels, mud or sand).
Location A claim, which see.
Lode claim A claim located on a lode, or solid rock, deposit.
Lode Deposit Mineralization contained within consolidated material (solid rock).
Long Tom A lengthy type of sluice box used in the early days.
Low Bench These are benches which have their gravels below the top of the adjacent valley bottom gravels.

Matrix The constituent minerals making up a rock.
Metal A single element of a class of substances such as gold, silver, copper, iron, lead etc.
Micron One millionth of a meter. (0.000001 meter).
Mineral A chemical combination of one element (metallic or otherwise) with another element or compound, to form a chemical identity, often called a mineral.

Mineralized A deposit which carries an above normal amount of mineral, such as pyrite, gold, uranium etc.
Mother Lode The main "lode" or ore deposit, within an auriferous region.

Native Gold Gold appearing without association with another metal. Can often be visually identified,
Nomad Matting A special type of floor matting put in sluice boxes for collection purposes.
Nugget Effect This is the coarse and uneven distribution of gold nuggets through a paystreak or lode. It gives rise to unusual effects in assaying.
Nugget Usually refers to gold the size of a grain of rice. Some are bigger-others smaller.

Open Pit In lode mining, it is a large pit from which mineralized rock formations are excavated
Outcrop A rock formation that is exposed on surface.
Outwash The material carried in a glacial meltwater stream and deposited as a buildup on a plain.
Overburden Useless material (such as dirt, sand) which overlies a bed of useful material (such as auriferous gravels).
Overflow The lighter material which rises with the water to the top and is drawn off.

Pay Gravels That thickness of placer gravel that carries economic gold values.
Paystreak The accumulation of gold values within placer gravels to form an economic zone.
Pediment A broad, gentle-sloping erosion surface found at the base of mountain fronts.
Pennyweight One-twentieth of a troy ounce. Old-fashion valuation system of gold,silver and jewels.

Placer Deposit A claim staked on a placer deposit in legal subdivisions generally 20 acres in size or roughly 1320 feet by 660 feet.

Plateau An erosional flat surface generally on uplifted ground.

Pleistocene A geological time frame within the Tertiary period. Runs from 100,000 years ago to 2 million years ago. The North American continent underwent four ice ages during this time which greatly altered the topography of the continent. As a matter of interest, it is during this ice period that man is thought to have evolved to his present form.

Porphyry Normally an intrusive rock containing large mineral crystals scattered through the matrix.

Productive Horizon That particular elevation, or location, within the gravels, or rock formation, which is economically mined.

Pyrite A mineral composed of iron and sulphur, occasionally auriferous.

Quartz A crystal, normally colorless or white, which forms quartz veins often associated with gold.

Ratio of Concentration The ratio of the weight of the feed compared to the weight of the concentrates.

Recovery The percentage of the gold in the ore that was collected in the concentrates.

Retorting A process involving distilling of the amalgam to recover the mercury and leave the sponge gold behind.

Rim Rock Rock outlining one of the banks of a buried channel.

Rocker A mechanical device to concentrate gold and black sands from placer gravels. Often used in dry washes.

Run Loose, unconsolidated, no cohesion. Referring to gravels.

Schist An altered rock that splits readily along specific planes.

Scour Surface The bedrock floor of a river channel that has been smoothed by rock action.

Settling Pond A quiet pond in which the fine gravels are allowed to settle to the bottom. The runoff from the sluices is often carried into this type of pond. The clean water may be recycled for further use.

Showing A surface rock exposure that carries mineralization (lode).

Silt Very fine rock particles which often form clay beds in gravels when deposited.

Sizing The grading into specific sizes by means of mesh screens.

Slimes A suspension of finely pulverised material, generally less than 10 microns in size, in water which upon drying becomes oozy mud.

Sluice Box A mechanical device to concentrate gold and black sands from placer gravels with the assistance of running water.

Slurry An aqueous solution carrying solid material in its flow.

Specific Gravity The relationship of a material's weight in air, under controlled conditions, compared to its weight in water.

Sphalerite An ore of zinc. Coupled with sulphur.

Tail Ditch A drainage ditch from concentrator to settling pond.

Tailings The end,waste, product or discharge from concentrating machines or mills. Presumably low in gold content.
Talus Broken rock fragments accumulating at the base of a slope.
Tenor Grade of a deposit, or sample, normally expressed (in placers) as ounces, or dollars, per cubic yard.
Terrace See bench.
Tertiary A time period in the geological clock which is from the end of the Cretaceous period to the present time (65 million years).

Underflow The heavier, sinking material which is drawn off along with a percentage of the water at the bottom of a unit (such as a jig).
Undersize That material which passes through the mesh of a screen for sizing purposes.
Uplift A geologic process which raises a surface section above the surrounding area.

Visible Gold See native gold. Often expressed as "V.G.".
Volcanic rock The flow material plus the ejected material that emerges from an active volcano.

Wash Loose alluvial material concentrated on desert pavements. May have intermittent stream action.
Weathering The erosional actions of the weathering agencies on surface structures.
Weight Combination of size and specific gravity.
Wing Dam An obstruction erected to run the surface waters from or to a placer operation. Sometimes called a shoofly dam.
Workings In a lode mine, it refers to the underground excavations. In a placer operation it refers to the area from where the gravels are being removed.

ARIZONA

With a population approaching 3.5 million and an area of 113,900 square miles, Arizona ranks sixth in size within the nation. It is home to one seventh of the United States Indian population. Twenty Indian reservations hosting 14 tribes occupy 19 million acres, one quarter of the state's area. The Navajo Nation, in the northeastern corner, is the largest reservation. One in six of Arizona's population is of Spanish ancestry, with the greatest density located in those counties bordering Mexico.

Geographically Arizona has distinctive regions. The north and northeast consist of plateaus (the great Colorado plateau), while the Nevadan basin and range design reaches into Arizona's southwest. Lying between these two geographical features is a broad band of mountain ranges.

One of Arizona's most persistent problems is its water supply. Two consistent rivers, the Colorado and the Gila have had dams (Hoover and Coolidge) erected to store precious water. Intermittent rivers such as the Verde, Agua Fria, San Pedro, Black, Salt (Roosevelt Dam), Little Colorado and the San Francisco help supply the state following the rainy seasons. The latter period occurs during July and August and the winter months.

Mining has always been first and foremost in Arizona's economy. The mills and refineries surrounding many cities are testimonial to the emphasis placed on this industry. Arizona ranks first in copper, production coming from the huge open pits such as at San Manuel, Hayden, Tucson, Morenci, and Miami among many.

Figure A-1: Arizona

Early history places the first working of Arizona placers at a location some 75 miles west of Tucson. Here a Spanish missionary with Indians is reported to have been active in

1774. The Gila River placers some 20 to 25 miles east of its junction with the Colorado were discovered in 1858. A discovery in 1862 by a cavalry officer led to the La Paz placers and eventually to others in the immediate vicinity. Most active time for placer mining was between 1858 and 1880. Since the turn of the century placer mining in Arizona has been an on-again, off-again affair depending upon the economy of the nation and the state.

Arizona has some 87 placer districts which are estimated to have produced in excess of 565,000 ounces of gold to 1968. A good percentage of the workings are of the dry variety. We will start with the eastern counties, moving next into the central counties, and finally checking out the western counties before entering California.

Cochise County

Located in the southeastern corner of the state, snuggled against New Mexico to the east and Mexico to the south. One of the earlier prospected counties with some large open pit copper mines operating at Courtland and Bisbee. Three relatively prominent placer situations are located at Dos Cabezas, Teviston and Huachuca mountains. Other minor occurrences lie near the Mexican border on the south flank of Mule Mountain (Gold Gulch), and off the eastern flank (Peace Hill) and the southeast end of Dragoon Mountain (Turquoise District) in the central section of the state.

District Name: Dos Cabezas and Teviston

Location: Dos Cabezas Mountains

General: The Dos Cabezas Mountains form a range extending northwestward between Bowie and Willcox off Interstate 10. The range extends some 20 miles in length, is 3 to 10 miles in width and is 6060 feet above sea level at their highest peak. The mountains are mineralized locally along a thrust fault zone known as the "Big Ledge". Four small gold mines operated intermittently on the "ledge" and adjacent gold-quartz veins.

Placer Possibilities: North Flank (Teviston Section) — Placers are found in mountain gulches and on mountain pediments. Little running water in this area so these placers are of the dry wash type. Productive gravels are said to extend from three to ten feet from the surface and one of the pediments is reported to have assayed 0.117 ounces gold per cubic yard ($41 @ $350 gold) over a six foot depth. The gold is of a coarse variety, thinning out as distance increases from the foot of the mountain. Past placer mining was concentrated between Gold Gulch and Ash Gulch. Some caliche has been found with gold values lying below the cement.

South Flank (Dos Cabezas Section)—Gold is said to be found in the dry gulches between Walnut Canyon and Howard Canyon. The gold bearing gravels thicken in the canyons in the southern section and carry gold whose characteristics are flat, ragged and coarse.

Nearest Camp Ground: **Willcox** — at Bonita Canyon — 26 sites - Operated by National Park Service. (602) 824-3560

Nearest Motel: **Willcox** — Best Western — 92 units, restaurant. (602)384-3556

Comfort Inn — 73 units, restaurant close by. (602) 384-4222

District Name: Hereford District

Location: Huachuca Mountains (Ash Canyon)

General: The Huachuca Mountain is a highly elevated (+8400 feet) range extending south-southeast for a distance of 25 miles and dwindling at the southeast end as it crosses the border. Its sharp elevations, particularly on the east front, give rise to abrupt canyons which harbor the intermittent creeks that flow into the San Pedro River.

surrounding the town of Greaterville. The gold is of the recent variety and in the early days (1875) the nuggets were displayed on the surface. Today you have to go deeper to find the gold.

Greaterville is at 5,280 foot elevation and has an annual average rainfall of greater than 14 inches which means the gulches run water during the rainy period. Wet panning and sluicing are in order if the ground is available for staking.

There are some 13 mineralized gulches in the 5 1/2 square miles surrounding Granite mountain. The gravel depth varies in the productive gulches from several feet to tens of feet. The gold is uniformly distributed throughout the bed. Gold values are also located in benches on side hills.

Placer Possibilities: The past productive gulches from north to south:

Empire Gulch; Chispa Gulch; Colorado Gulch; Los Pogos Gulch; Hughes Gulch; Ophir Gulch: Nigger Gulch; Louisiana Gulch; Graham Gulch; Sucher Gulch; Harshav Gulch; Kentucky Gulch; Boston Gulch.

Nearest Campground: **Green Valley**

Bog Springs — open all year — at 5,000 foot elevation —13 sites — 22 foot RV limit — Forestry Service — (602) 281-2296.

Sonita

Lakeview — open all year — at 5,400 feet elevation — 64 sites — 32 foot RV limit — Forestry Service — (602) 458-0530.

Amado

Mountain View Campground — open all year — at 3,100 feet elevation — 100 sites — (602) 398-9401.

Nearest Motel: **Green Valley**

Quality Inn — 108 units — (602) 625-2250.

District Name: Arivaca District
Placer Name: Las Guijas Placers

Location: In southern Pima County off the flanks of the Las Guijas Mountains. The village of Arivaca is located 20 miles west of Arivaca Junction on I-19.

General: There were 3 localities in the foothills of the mountains that received attention in the past:

Northeast flank — just south of the little village of Las Guijas on the pediment slope, the gravels carry evenly distributed gold values over a distance of 2 1/2 miles and a width of 1 mile. A little further southeast in the gulches of Durzano and Pesqueria more gold has been located. Heavy black sands and a little mercury in the form of cinnabar accompany the gravels.

Southern slopes — in the large basins and wide arroyos just north of Arivaca Wash.

San Luis Canyon — short distance west of Arivaca. Bench gravels located on the mountain pediment.

Placer Possibilities: One of the earliest known placers. Placering using both the dry and wet methods has been a standard occupation in this locality. Check for any open ground. Las Guijas Creek yielded gold in the early days. Might be a place to pan.

Nearest Campground: **Amado**

See previously — 20 miles to the east of Arivaca.

Nogales

Patagonia Lake State Park — 42 miles via Highway 289 to Arivaca — open all year — 82 sites — RV limit 30 feet — (602) 287-6965.

Nearest Motel: **Nogales**

Motel Time (Best Western) — 42 units — (602) 287-4627.

Siesta Motel (Best Western) — 47 units — (602) 287-4671.

District Name: Quijotoa District

Placer Name: Quijotoa Placers

Location: East and west flanks of the Quijotoa Mountains in the Papago Indian Reserve. Quijotoa is 82 miles west of Tucson via Highway 86.

General: The placers are widely distributed and have been known and operated for a long time. The desert area (Horseshoe Basin) surrounding the village of Quijotoa has been mined for placers while several gulches known as Homestake and Midas some 3 miles to the north of the village have given up desert gold. All the mining is done by dry washing. Caliche is quite common in the area.

Placer Possibilities: The area has been mined for several centuries. In addition you are operating on Indian land. Occasional dry panning might be all right but it might be wise to investigate the land opportunities before becoming involved.

Nearest Campground: **Organ Pipe National Monument Park**, some 62 miles to the west. This is a Headquarters Campground, open all year with some 208 sites. RV limit is 35 feet. Operated by the National Parks Service — (602) 387-6849

Lukeville

Gringo Pass RV Park — open all year — 120 sites — (602) 254-9284

Nearest Motel: **Ajo**

La Siesta Motel — 10 units — (602) 387-6569

Marine Motel — 20 units — (602) 387-7626

Pinal County

Pinal County consists of extensive desert plains with a scattering of old mountain chains. The county has seen a moderate intensity of gold mining over the last 150 years with the emphasis being on lode mines. There is only one placer area of interest and it is not associated with any of the producing lode gold mines.

District Name: Old Hat District

Placer Name: Canada Del Oro Placers

Figure A-2: Panning in Arizona (1936)

Location: Along the northwest and northeast flanks of the Santa Catalina Mountains. Spur roads lead from Oracle into the placer areas on both flanks of the mountains.

General: The placer area lies in a large alluvial fan at the northwest end of the Santa Catalina Mountains. The dry gravels, reputed to carry more or less well-distributed gold, range in thickness from 6 feet at the Canada Del Oro Creek to a depth exceeding 300 feet where they emerge from the mountains. The creek is reported to carry values in the form of small nuggets over a wide width.

The northeast section of the flank has run values in the creek beds with the gold concentrated as a pay streak lying on a red clay base.

Placer Possibilities: Although these placer workings reportedly extend back to the Spanish days, it appears that values are still being extracted from them. Check all creeks for colors then check for ownership.

Nearest Campground: **Oracle**

Peppersauce — open all year — 31 sites — RV limit: 22 feet — National Forests (602) 629-5113.

Nearest Motel: **Tucson** (numerous motels)

Days Inn — Downtown — 159 units — (602) 622-4000

Holiday Inn — Downtown — 309 units-(602) 624-8711

Wayward Winds Lodge — Outskirts — 41 units — (602) 791-7526.

* * *

Maricopa County

One of the most densely populated counties in Arizona primarily because it includes the fastest growing city in America, Phoenix. The county is one of the more arid regions of Arizona having an average summer temperature of 110° F with an annual rainfall of 10.5 inches or less. Maricopa

County consists of broad desert plains with scattered mountain ranges.There are two well recognized placer areas in this county.

District Name: Vulture Mining District.

Placer Names: Red Top Basin and Vulture Wash.

Location: In northwestern Maricopa County on the south flank of the Vulture Mountains.

General: These placers appear to be the result of the erosion of the Vulture mine veins. Some early high grade material was discovered in these diggings.

Placer Possibilities: A few miles west of Wickenburg on US-60, an improved road leads some 14 miles southwest over the mountains in the general direction of the Vulture Mine.

Red Top Basin —This is a pediment placer deposit within the basin to the northwest of the old mine site. Although the gravels are relatively thin (less than 10 feet) there is considerable caliche cement associated with them. Before beginning extended operations here check as to the ownership of the land. Elevation is approx. 2500'.

Vulture Wash —Some 4 miles further along the road and directly below the mine site, this wash extends some 2 miles to the south east. Again the cemented gravels are thin and the gold reportedly coarse and angular showing a short travel distance. Elevation is about 2000 feet.

Nearest Campground: **Aquila**

Fairhaven RV Park — open all year — 55 sites — (602) 685-2412.

Nearest Motels: **Wickenburg**

American Motor Inn — 29 units — (602) 684-5461.

Best Western Rancho Grande Motel — 80 units — (602) 684-5445.

District Name: San Domingo District

Placer Names: San Domingo Wash, Little San Domingo

Wash, Old Woman Gulch, Rogues Wash, American Gulch, and Spring Gulch.

Location: The Hieroglyphic Mountains (locally called Wickenburg Mountains)lie on the northeast side of US 60 and 93. About 4 miles north of Morristown, several gravel roads lead up to San Domingo Wash which is an intermittent tributary of the underground Hassayampa Creek.

General : This wash has numerous tributaries which coupled with the adjacent washes and the mesas separating the gulches has yielded rich finds in the past. The mountain front running northwest from San Domingo Wash has been productive and should still offer good possibilities. Dry washing tho'!

Placer Possibilities: All the washes and gulches along this front are deserving of attention. There has been a good amount of past production from this area.Gold is reported near bedrock in the upper reaches (particularly in the mesas) where the gravel is thin but becomes more distributed down the washes as the gravels thicken.

Nearest Campground: See previous on Aquila.

Nearest Motels: See previous on Wickenburg.

* * *

Yavapai County

Located in mid-central Arizona this 8,150 square mile county ranks number one among the gold-producing counties of Arizona. It is also the leader in the placer production. The large copper producer at Jerome has materially contributed to the gold production.

Geologically the county consists of a series of northward and northwestward trending fault block mountain ranges and valleys. Placers have been worked in more than 30 locations in the county being concentrated on the slopes of the Bradshaw and associated Mountains often close to small hard rock deposits.

District Name: Weaver Mining District

Figure A-3: Panning in Arizona (1913)

Placer Names: Weaver and Rich Hill Placers
Location: In south-central Yavapai County. A mile north of Congress on U.S. 89, then on to gravel road 6 1/2 miles south to Stanton. Located on southern edge of Weaver Mountains. Richhill Mountain, several miles east of Stanton, has Antelope Creek on west side, and Weaver Creek on east side, both rich placer creeks.
General: One of the earliest Arizona placer discoveries. A placer field at the top of Richhill mountain was likely the result of an elevated pediment. The sides of the hill and both creeks — Weaver and Antelope — have placer material in the gravels.

These gravels have been re-worked many times.

Placer Possibilities: Both creeks run intermittent and have heavy duty placer operations established. However the past richness of the area makes a gamble well worthwhile. Check carefully for open ground.

Nearest Campground: **Prescott**

Four Forestry Service operated camp sites, all with 32 foot RV limit. (602) 445-7253.

Granite Basin — 18 sites.

Indian Creek — 27 sites, open May to September.

Lower Wolf Creek — 20 sites, open May to November.

White Spar — 62 sites — slight charge.

Point of Rocks Campground — open all year — 100 sites — private — (602) 445-9018

Nearest Motel: **Wickenburg** (which see.)

District Name: Walker and Bigbug Districts

Placer Name: Prescott Placers

Location: Some 7 to 10 miles southeast of Prescott in the wooded, well watered north and northeast slope of the Bradshaw Mountains.

General: Two areas of interest:

1. Lynx Creek — the upper portion in the mountains (6000 feet above sea level) has been sluice and rocker mined numerous times, each time yielding gold values. The gold occurs in thin gravels or narrow benches or bars.

The lower part of the creek parallels Highway 69 and is in Lonesome Valley. Gold deposited in late alluvium from 8 to 25 feet thick near the bottom of steep gulches.

2. Big Bug Creek — Roads from highway 69 at Humboldt and Mayer lead south to this creek. The most productive parts of this creek were the stream gravels of upper Big Bug Creek;

tributary gulches such as Eugene and Chaparral and gravel benches near Mayer.

Placer Diggings, Lynx Creek

Placer Possibilities: Although reworked several times, these placers have never failed to yield colors. It would be well to check out these streams then check for ownership if deemed worthwhile. This is one of the more scenic areas of Arizona with a pleasant mountain climate.

Nearest Campground: **Dewey**

Powel Springs — open all year — 10 sites — RV limit: 22 feet — Forestry Service (602) 567-4121.

Prescott See previous.

Nearest Motel: **Prescott**

Prescottonian Motel (Best Western) — open all year — 121 units — (602) 445-3096.

Super 8 Motel — open all year —70 units —(602) 776-1282.

Sierra Inn — open all year — 49 units — (602) 445-1250.

Other placer areas of interest in Yanapai County are:

Hassayampa River — Placer mined from Wickenburg upstream (42 miles) to Groom Creek.

Black Canyon — Highway 69 which parallels I-17 between Bumblebee and Black Canyon City.

Model Creek — Both Model and Kirkland Creek in Peeples Valley have been placered. Area is near Kirkland Junction.

* * *

Yuma County

Yuma County, the most southwesterly of the 15 countries, is probably the most arid of the counties with broad desert plains and north northwestward trending fault block mountains.Only the Colorado and Gila rivers provide perennial running water through the area. The climate is uncomfortable for placer mining during the summer as maximum temperature during this season at Yuma may reach 118°. The mean annual rainfall is slightly more than 3 inches.

There are two relatively important placer areas in Yuma County.

District Name: Dome District

Placer Name: Gila City

Location: At the north end of the Gila Mountains in the vicinity of Dome. The placers are located south of the Gila River extending southward into the gulches and up the mountain pediment.

General: The discovery of these gravels goes back to 1858 and they have been repeatedly reworked. They were very rich gravels and have yielded colors when reworked. The placers are of the dry washing type due to lack of water. The outwash scattered in the gulches and on benches has yielded values in the past.
Placer Possibilities: This could be a good place to work during the wet season. The concentrate from dry washing could be rewashed on the Gila River banks. As this area is close to the U.S. Army Restricted Proving Ground be careful of your location, although I'm sure the Army will let you know if you're on their ground!
Nearest Campground: **Yuma**

Araby Acres Travel Trailer Park — 338 sites — open from Oct. to May — (602) 344-8666.

Bonita Mesa — open all year — 586 sites — (602) 342-2999.

Rogers RV Resort — open all year — 720 sites — (602) 342-2992.

Nearest Motel: **Yuma**

Coronado Motor Hotel (Best Western) — 49 units — (602) 783-4453.

Yuma 4th Ave. (Travelodge) — 48 units — (602) 782-3831.

Yuma Cabara Motel — 63 units — (602) 783-8311.

District Name: Cactus Dome District
Placer Name: Castle Dome Placers
Location: On the southwest flank of the Castle Dome Mountains in the Kofa National Wildlife Refuge, some 28 miles northeast of Yuma on US 95. Here a gravel road travels east some 12 miles to the edge of the mountains then heads north along washes.
General: The early recovery of gold was mostly at or near bedrock in gulches off the Big Eye Wash. The location is closeby an old gold mine appropriately called the Big Eye

Mine. Recovery from the gravels is mostly by dry washing due to the scarcity of water.

Placer Possibilities: The location of these placers is very poorly defined. Best to locate the Big Eye Mine and then check the gravels in the gulches on the downslope side of mountain. Remember it's dry washing here.

Nearest Campground: See Yuma previously.

Nearest Motel: See Yuma previously.

Other placer areas in Yuma County include Laguna, Muggins, Kofa and Tank Mountains.

* * *

La Paz

In 1984, the county of La Paz was created out of Yuma County. Parker on the Colorado river at the California border was designated the county seat. An old mining town, Quartzite on I-10, was the site of early historical mining activity which included lode and placer discoveries. However some of the later blooming placers operated out of this county. The county comprises an area encompassing roughly 5,600 square miles of desert plains and north-northwestward trending fault-block mountains. The only permanent flowing waters are the Williams and the Colorado rivers.

District Name: Plomosa

Placer Name: Two placer areas called La Cholla and Plomosa.

Location: The Plomosa placers lie at the eastern edge of the La Posa plain on a pediment of the Plomosa Mountains, some five miles southeast of Quartzite; while the La Cholla area comprises three adjacent placers, also pediment located, bordering the eastern foot of the Dome Rock Mountains astride I- 10 (12 miles west of the Plomosa Camp).

General: Most of the placer areas are within easy reach of I-10. Numerous side roads lead off to the placer sites which are, in this area, primarily dry washes. The placers lie at the north end of a military restricted area.

Placer Possibilities: La Cholla —This placer camp consists of three individually located but close by areas called La Cholla (south of I-10), Oro Fino (just north of I-10) and Middle Camp (immediately north of the Oro Fino).These camps are all small-scale, dry washers with values reportedly running in the $4 to $6 per cubic yard category. The gravels are thick.

La Plomosa —Placer areas located in old drainage channels in the vicinity of Plomosa Wash. Gravels are of variable thickness and reputedly ran in the $3 to $5 per cubic yard evaluation. Mostly dry washing.

Nearest Campground: **Quartzite** — B-10 Campground — 110 sites — open November to April 15th — adjacent to I-10 (602) 927-4393

La Posa Long Term Visitor Area — 2000 sites — BLM operated — open October to May 1st — (602) 726-6300.

Nearest Motel: **Blythe** (in California)

Best Western Sahara Motel — 47 units — (619) 922-7105.
Blythe Travelodge — 50 units — (619) 922-5145.
Comfort Inn — 48 units — (619) 922-4146.

District Name: La Paz Placers

Location: Along western foot of the Dome Rock mountains, 9 miles west of Quartzite. North of I-10.

General: Several small arroyos drain westward to the Colorado river. An old adobe town, called La Paz, was established in 1863. Today it is a ghost town. The placers are very close to the Indian reservation.

Placer Possibilities: Most of the past operations proceeded in Goodman and La Paz Arroyos. In addition tributary gulches such as Ferrar, Garcia and Ravenna contributed to the placers wealth. The gravels, again a pediment deposit, are said to be up to 60 feet deep. Remember lack of water forces dry washing. Check ownership.

Nearest Campground: **Blythe, CA**

5 campgrounds open all year, varying from 15 to 235 RV sites.

Coon Hollow — BLM — 29 sites
Mayflower Park — Private — (619) 922-4665.
McIntyre Park — Private — (619) 922-8205.
Riviera Blythe Marina — Private — (619) 922-5350.
Wiley Well — Private — (619) 323-4421.

Nearest Motel: **Blythe, CA** (See previous).

District Name: Trigo Placers.

Location: Along western base of the Trigo mountains, at Cibola located 20 miles south of Ehrenberg.

General: Several dry washes from the Trigo mountains drain westward into the nearby Colorado River. A wash 4 miles southeast of Cibola has been actively worked while the Colorado River flood sands some 13 miles south of Cibola has yielded gold to Depression era miners.

Placer Possibilities: At Cibola small scale dry washing of the arroyo gravels has been relatively active. The Colorado River sands at Paradise Valley, 15 miles south of Cibola, have demonstrated gold values in the past.

The Chocolate Mountain washes to the southeast of Cibola were actively placered during the Depression years but this range is in a highly restricted military area at the present time.

* * *

Mohave County

Mohave county ranks second in the state to gold production with 90% coming from the lode gold mines, while the estimated placer production places it seventh among the eleven producing counties. This county, composed of some 16,150 square miles, has 20% of it in the northeastern portion contained within the Colorado Plateau, while the remainder is given over to the faulted mountain and valley complex extending in from Nevada.

The gold districts are mostly in the most central part of the county lying within close proximity to the lode producing mines. No gold districts occur within the Colorado Plateau.There are two well recognized placer areas in Mohave county.

District Name: Lost Basin District
Placer Name: 1) Gold Basin Placers and 2) King Tut Placers
Location: From a point 39 miles northwest of Kingman on US-93 a gravel road runs westward into the White Hills, passes below Cyclopic, on through the Lost Basin Range and down to Pierce Ferry. The Gold Basin placers lie within the detrital fan sloping eastward from the White Mountains into Hualapai Wash, while the King Tut Placers are found along the east flank of the Lost Basin Range. The Gold Basin placers lie due north of Cyclopie and the King Tut lies over (eastward) the Lost Basin Range.
General: These placer areas were late in discovery being initially worked during the depression years.

In the Gold Basin, the arroyos and gulches branching into the fan have been the most productive with placer gravels averaging from one to 3 feet thick and resting upon a bedrock of caliche-cemented gravels. The erratically distributed gold ranges from fine to coarse. It has tested as high as $10 per cubic yard but generally is much lower than that. The fan extending some 6 miles into Hualapai Wash is crossed by the White Elephant Wash and its tributaries.

Both areas are of the dry wash variety.

Placer Possibilities: Late in being introduced to the placer world, the Lost Basin District placers might still carry gold values of consequence. Check out ownership of the ground if you contemplate extended operations.

Nearest Campground: **Kingman**

Adobe RV Park — open all year — private —75 sites — (602) 565-3010.

Hualapai Mt. Park — open all year —county run — 11 RV sites — (602) 757-3859.

Kingman KOA — open all year — privately run — reserve deposit — 97 sites — (602) 757-4397.

Nearest Motel: **Kingman**

Best Western King's Inn — 53 units — restaurant nearby — (602) 753-6101.

Days Inn — 60 units — closeby restaurant — (602) 753-7500.

District Name: Gold Wing District

Placer Name: Chemehuevis Placers

Location: Located on the northeast and southwestern flanks of the the Mohave mountains. Highway 95 traverses these mountains on the way to Lake Havasu City from off I-40.

General: These placers had the greatest work done during the depression period. The gravels are angular, not having travelled far, and at depths are cemented by carbonates. Simililarly the gold is coarse. Gravels shown to vary from 0.06 to 0.165 ounces gold per cubic yard (at $350, $21.00 to $57.50). These are dry wash placers.

Placer Possibilities: Northeastern end — At Dutch and Printers Gulches — some 5 miles on Highway 96 then along the front on gravel roads for a distance of 5 to 6 miles.

Southwestern end — At a point where the highway comes down from the mountains, an old channel called Calizona at one time flowed out of the mountains towards the Colorado River. The channel, buried below 10 to 30 feet of gravel, flows northwest for 3 to 5 miles and has a width of 1 mile. It may be well to find tributaries which flowed into this ancient channel.

Some 4 to 5 miles further south, near an area called the Red Hills, placer activity took place at a showing called the Mexican or Spanish diggings.

Closest Campground: **Lake Havasu City**

Crazy Horse Campground — open all year — 615 sites — (602) 855-4033.

Cat-Tail Cove — in State park — open all year — 40 sites — 30 foot RV limit — (602) 855-1223.

Nearest Motel: **Lake Havasu City**

Lake Place Inn (Best Western)— 40 units — (602) 855-2146.

Holiday Inn — 163 units — (602) 855-4071

Lake Havasu City (Super 8) — 60 units — (602) 855-8844.

District Name: Oatman Mining District

Placer Name: Silver Creek Placers

Location: Oatman is about 30 miles southeast of Kingman on Highway 66. The placers are found along the western slopes of the southern portion of the Black Mountains. This is the richest lode gold mining area in Mohave County.

General: Three areas of interest:

1. Small tributaries into Silver Creek Wash, an intermittent stream, just north of Mount Hardy. Variable size gold in gravels on a pediment. The valley of Silver Creek further to the northwest has also yielded gold values.

Figure A-5: Arizona Rocker

2. Two miles north of Silver Creek Wash, the Moss vein was located. The gravels below this vein are reported to have carried coarse gold.

3. A small stream just below the Pioneer mine has been sluiced in the past yielding values. This is 1.5 miles south of Oatman.

Placer Possibilities: Gulches, which are dry except during the rainy seasons, carry the run off from the side of the mountains westward to the Colorado River. A few small perennial springs issue from beds, particularly in Silver Creek.

In the past most of these areas have been worked by dry placering. The intriguing point is that sluicing in certain areas was done during the winter season when water was running in the gulches, therefore the area can be wet placered. Note the phrase "during the winter season". That part of Arizona between the Colorado River and the adjoining mountains is "hell on wheels" during the summer months!

Nearest Campground: **Bullhead City**

Riverview RV Resort — open all year — 697 sites — (602) 763-5800.

Bullhead RV Park — open all year — 156 sites — (602) 763-8355.

Kingman, which see.

Nearest Motel: **Bullhead City**

Grand Vista Hotel (Best Western) — 80 units — (602) 763-3300

Holiday Inn — 155 units — (602) 754-4700.

Silver Creek Inn — 68 units — (602) 763-8400

We are now ready to enter the exciting State of California!!

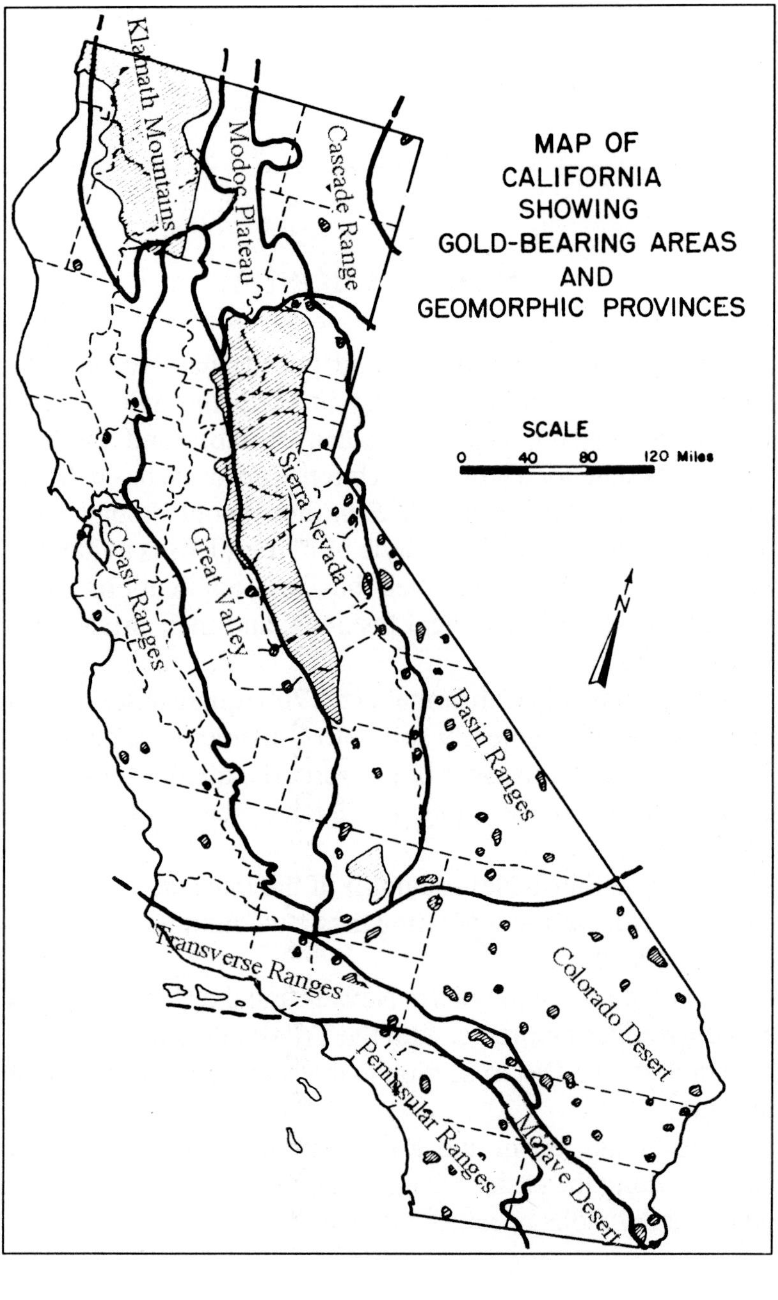
MAP OF
CALIFORNIA
SHOWING
GOLD-BEARING AREAS
AND
GEOMORPHIC PROVINCES
SCALE
0 40 80 120 Miles
N
Klamath Mountains
Modoc Plateau
Cascade Range
Sierra Nevada
Coast Ranges
Great Valley
Basin Ranges
Transverse Ranges
Colorado Desert
Peninsular Ranges
Mojave Desert

CALIFORNIA

"The Land of Opportunity" and indeed it has lived up to its name. From its initial discovery in 1542, through its early allegiance to Spain, on to its Mexican affiliation and finally in 1850 to its statehood within the Union, California has held out expectations which some 28.5 million people today have developed into a distinctive style of living. This is evident in their varied architecture, their business applications, their bourgeois art, their classical fashions, and their mixed cuisines.

Geographically California's 158,700 square miles of land mass can be conveniently spilt into 6 distinctive sections:
1) The mountainous areas of the north (Klamath Mountains) coupled with those along the Pacific seaboard (Coastal Mountains).
2) The great Sierra Nevada uplift of the interior.
3) The fertile valley separating these two mountain areas — the Great Valley.
4) The blending of the Sierra Nevada and the Coastal ranges at their southern extremes into the Transverse range.
5) The Mohave Desert section in the southeastern section of the state
6) The Great Basin and Range complex extending from Nevada along the eastern front of the Sierras. There are four other subdivisions of minor interest.

California's reputation as a land of opportunity sprang from the gold rush of 1849. The influx of "miners" from states other than California grew as the legend of the gold finds became a reality. Struggling through a lawless period of the gold fever, Californians witnessed new settlements springing up only to become ghost towns within the next few decades. They saw the golden era die out to be replaced by more concrete and permanent signs. They ushered in the competition of the transcontinental railways, which brought business and industry from the central plains and eastern seaboard. They developed the irrigation needs of the Great Valley and, moreover, these actions brought in the type of settlers more interested in the future development of a great state.

The gold fever has gone. However many towns associated with it have survived and continue to provide services for the itinerant prospector who knows full well "all the gold is not gone".

California leads all the states in gold placer production. A relatively recent report lists California as having processed some 68,200,000 troy ounces of placer gold. While most of this production has come, and still comes, from the Sierra Nevadas, contributors in the past and present are the Klamath Mountains, the Mohave Desert and the Basin and Range complex.

California is rich in its gold deposits, both lode and placer. Coupled with the lode deposits the state has contributed 106 million troy ounces of gold. In California the areas of known gold deposition are referred to as districts. A district has no set limits and, indeed, might blend into an adjoining district.

In addition, California is unique, as opposed to Nevada and Arizona, in having so many Tertiary deposits. This is specially true of the Sierra Nevadas where the uplift of this tremendous mountain range, followed by volcanic outpourings and eventual erosion has materially altered and buried the path of the ancestral rivers. The tracing and mining of these buried Tertiary channels has given birth to many drift miners of yesterday and today.

Until 1884 California permitted hydraulic action on hillsides containing Tertiary deposits. However a court action in that year ended this type of operation and, although permitted in later years, it never came back to prominence.

There are 38 known gold counties in California which collectively have over 140 mining districts. These are listed under their geographic section and, where that particular county contained multiple districts, for brevity's sake, I have located only one or two camping areas or accommodation sites which I feel is central to all. This is particularly true in the Sierra Nevadas where each county is a complete treasure house of RV gold hunting in itself due to the numerous districts.Because of the multiplicity of gold districts I have eliminated the commentary on each county and, similarly I have done away with the district write-ups.

Klamath Mountain Province

The Klamath Mountain region in northwestern California is the second-most gold productive province in California. The area consists of a number of complex and rugged mountain ranges that continue north into Oregon. While there are some lode gold districts, the placer deposits have been the largest supplier of gold. The principal placer gold districts are in Shasta, Siskiyou and Trinity counties and are primarily associated with the Klamath and Trinity Rivers plus their tributaries.

The most important tributary streams of the Klamath River are the Shasta, Scott, and Salmon Rivers while the Cottonwood, Horse, Seiad, Thompson, Indian, Clear, Dillon and Camp are the placer creeks.

The Trinity River, which flows into the Klamath River at Weitchpec, has as tributaries Coffee Creek, Stewart's Fork, East Fork, New River, Indian Creek and Hayfork Creek.

Gold is found in the gravels of the present stream channels of the two rivers and, additionally, in older terrace and bench deposits adjacent to the Klamath River.

The Klamath Mountain area has mined some $242 million is gold since the original discovery.

Siskiyou County

The most northerly of the counties in California and the Klamath Mountain region. It directly adjoins the State of Oregon.

If we follow the Klamath River downstream (SW to west) from where it enters California from Oregon, we travel US Interstate I5 to Hornbrook

Cottonwood Creek. This creek empties into the Klamath at Hornbrook.During the days of the '49 Rush, this was an extremely rich creek.Check it out now by panning it back up creek.

Shasta River. At a point 5 miles south of Hornbrook,where highway 96 goes west to follow the Klamath River, the Shasta empties into the Klamath. Both the Shasta and two of its tributaries, Yreka Creek and Greenhorn Creek (several miles south) are reputed to have yielded large amounts of gold.

If we travel along highway 96, which closely follows the Klamath River, we come to the

Humbug Creek. 3 miles west on #96 where this creek empties into the Klamath. Reported to have been very rich during the rush.

Continuing west we meet up with the first major tributary at Hamburg — the Scott River. A road follows up (south) this river.

Scotts Bar. At a location three miles up creek we enter the Scotts Bar District. Aptly named for an auriferous gravel bar that extended across the river. Check the bench gravels in this vicinity.

Deadwood District. At Fort Jones, 27 miles further upstream, Moffett Creek empties into the Scott. Follow highway 3 several miles up Moffett Creek to where a number of small creeks (Deadwood, Cherry, Indian, French and McAdam) meet the main stream. Good placer results were had from these creeks in past years.

Figure C-2: Northern Operation

Oro Fino District. Going south on #3 road from Fort Jones we encounter the Oro Fino district. This includes Quartz Valley and Mugginsville area. The creeks running down

Quartz Hill have carried gravels with the gold particles being fine but rough and angular, showing a short distance of travel.

Callahan District. 20 miles along the upper Scott River brings us into the Callahan district. Here bench gravels and tributary gulches previously yielded good gold results.Bucket line dredges have worked this section of the river. Expect weak gold results.

Returning to the Klamath River and continuing along highway #96, we follow a major placer mining situation.All the tributary creeks, Masonic, Skeahan, Oak Bar, Beaver, Horse, Lumgrey, Empire and Dutch, plus Kanaka Bar and Gottsville, all saw extensive placer operations.

Continuing westward along the river, numerous hydraulic and dredge areas appear at Seiad Valley and Happy Valley.

Indian Creek District. A gravel road follows this creek northwest from #96. Good gold results are reported from this creek.The road is closed in the winter season.

Dillon Creek District. This mining district some 26 miles further south along # 96 saw extensive operations during the '49 rush and the Depression years. There is sporadic mining in the area.

Somes Bar. Fifteen miles south of Dillon Creek is where the Salmon River empties into the Klamath. The Klamath continues on south into Humboldt county.

Forks of Salmon District. A county road from Somes Bar follows the Salmon River 17 miles upstream to the junction of the two rivers. A tremendous amount of dredging has been done where the North and South Forks meet.

Sawyer's Bar. Some 16 miles up the North Fork from Forks. This was an extremely rich river placer mining area in past years. Try a few pans here. Any streams flowing into this creek should be checked.

Liberty District. Some 9 miles south of Sawyer's Bar in the Salmon Mountains. This is a difficult area to get into but there are numerous creeks worth investigation.

Snowden District. This is a further 6 miles up the North Fork. Many sections along this stretch of the river were worked by wingdams and flumes following the hand methods,panning and rockering.

Knownothing. 9 miles up the South Fork. Past reports show good gold mineralization in the available gravels.

Cecilville. 10 miles beyond Knownothing. near the junction of the East and South Forks of the Salmon. Gold discovered in 1849 with thousands of people migrating to the area. Later reworked by the Chinese.

Callahan—We have now come full cycle around the Salmon Mountains.This is a journey of 315 miles including the return mileages. The various interest points could well be covered from staying at one or two of the following campsites.

Campgrounds: ***Callahan*** —

Trail Creek — May 28 to October 15 — 15 sites — National Forests (916) 468-5351.

Cecilville —

Shadow Creek — June 1 to October 15 — 10 sites — National Forests (916) 467-5757.

Happy Camp —West Branch — May 1 to October 31 — 10 sites — National Forests (916) 493-2243.

Sawyers Bar — Idlewild — May 27 to November 30 — 23 sites — National Forests (916) 467-5757.

Somes Bar — Dillon Jim — Open all year — 21 sites — National Forests — (916) 469-3331.

Oak Bottom — Open all year — 56 sites — National Forests — (916) 469-3331.

Yreka — Tree of Heaven — May 15 to November 1 — 21 sites — National Forests (916) 465-2241.

Waiiaka Trailer Haven — all year — 64 sites — Private — (916) 842-4500.

Motels: ***Happy Camp*** — Forest Lodge Motel — Open all year — 15 units (916) 842-4355

Yreka — Miners Inn (Best Western) — Open all year — 91 units — (916) 842-4355.

Thunderbird Lodge — Open all year — 44 units — (916) 842-4402.

Humboldt County

This county directly adjoins Siskiyou County on the southwest. The county also borders on the Pacific Ocean front. With Del Norte county it shares the world famous Redwood National Park. Although several rivers (Mad, Van Duzen, Mattole) empty into the Pacific they do not have the placer history as is attached to the Klamath, and its major tributary, the Trinity River.

Somes Bar — The Klamath River flows southwestward for some 24 miles. Check the small creeks flowing out of the mountains into this river.

Orlean — Located ten miles below Somes Bar on the river. The older bench gravels some 50 to 75 feet above the present river level have been productive in the past as has been the present river gravels. Platinum is reported in the gravels along with fine to medium gold particles.

Weitchpec — Some 14 miles further downstream, the Trinity river empties into the Klamath. The Trinity has been placer mined in numerous localities and its point of entry into the Klamath makes for some interesting panning localities a few miles further down stream.

At this point, the Klamath turns northwest and 45 miles further along empties into the Pacific Ocean at Requa in Del Norte county.

If we follow the Trinity upstream we will eventually pass into Trinity county.

Trinity County

This county lies directly south of Siskiyou and to the east of Humboldt county. It hosts the Trinity River one of the major tributaries of the Klamath. The Trinity River lies at the southwestern edge of the Salmon mountains and numerous creeks and streams issuing out of these mountains have carried gold values. However we also pass through numerous old placer areas. So lets head south from Weitchpec on Highway 96.

Hoopa — This old placer mining country, some 12 miles upstream, is in the Hoopa Indian Reservation. The present river gravels will yield colors as will the older terrace benches above the river.

At Willow Creek, a further 11 miles, we pick up Route 299 and head southeast, still following the Trinity River.

Salyer — The river splits here into a south and main branch. Amazingly the south branch has little recorded placer history. It follows along the east base of the South Forks Mountain.

At Salyer, bench gravels above the main Trinity river have shown colors in past placer operations.

New River — The New River empties into the main Trinity 5 miles up from Salyer. A county road leads northeast from here through New River on to Denny. Both of these areas have reputations for good placering.

Continuing southeast on 299 we pass through Burnt Ranch, Big Barn and Helena, and on to **Junction City,** a distance of 45 miles from Willow Creek. This is the site of extensive dredge operations. Names associated with the hydraulic bench operations here are Coopers Bar, Hocker Flat,Benjamin Flat and Chapman Ranch.

A county road here leads north to Dedrick allowing access to Canyon Creek and Oregon Gulch. Check these areas out.

Figure C-3: Active Sluices

Weaverville — 10 miles beyond Junction City is the junction of Highways 3 and 299. This area has seen a great deal of hydraulicking action in earlier days.

Now if we travel north on highway 3 from Weaverville we pass through **Trinity Creek** and **Carrville,** both on the Trinity Rivers system, and both historically famous as placer deposits. Check all the creeks entering the main river, particularly *Coffer Creek* at Carrville and *Swift Creek* at Trinity Centre.

At ***Lewiston,*** 11 miles east of Douglas City and just off Highway 299, and at Eastman Gulch, 5 miles further, both areas have yielded high grade gold values in past operations from tributary streams.

Returning to Weaverville and travelling south here we pass through Douglas City, a distance of 7 miles. The tributary creeks Weaver, Indian and Reading are known for good production. Investigate these creeks. If colors show, check the possibility of claims.

Continuing south to ***Hayfork***, a further distance of 23 miles, we locate ourselves on a tributary of the south fork of the Trinity River. A great deal of dragline dredging and hydraulic action was carried on here. The streams entering this tributary make interesting gold panning.

Campgrounds : ***Hoopa*** Tish Tang — June 1 to November 1 — 40 sites — National Forests — (916) 629-2118

Salyer — Lazy Double B RV Park — all year — 46 sites — Private — (916) 629-2156

Big Bar — Hayden Flat — July 1 to October 1 — 35 sites — National Forests — (916) 623-6106

Weaverville — Minersville — all year — 21 sites — National Forests — (916) 623-2131.

Trinity Centre — Alpine View — May 15 to September 15 — 66 sites — National Forests — (916) 623-2121.

Motels: ***Hoopa —*** Tsewenaldin Inn (Best Western) — 22 units — Restaurant — (916) 625-4294.

Douglas City — Indian Creek Lodge — 14 units — (916) 623-6294.

Weaverville — Motel Trinity — 25 units — (916) 623-2129.

* * *

Shasta County

Like Trinity, this county bounds Siskiyou on the south end and lies directly east of Trinity county. Most of the placer workings are in the southwestern part of the county.

Continuing east on 299 from our visit to Lewiston we cross the county line at Backhorn Summit and some 5 miles further along follow a county road north to French Gulch, one of the more important gold producing areas in the Klamath Mountain. Some 38 mines existed here at one time and it is estimated the area produced in excess of $30 million of gold. Check Trail Gulch, Sawpit Gulch, Summit Gulch, French Gulch and Cline Gulch all of which empties into Clear Creek, at one time a prolific placer creek. ***Whiskey Town***, a ghost town, lies six miles further along on 299. Clear Creek meanders through the town and continues on through to Shasta then south. County road A-16 leads off 299 to *Ono* and *Igo*, two well recognized placer areas. Check out the stream gravels in Clear Creek, also Eagles, North Cottonwood and Dry Creeks. The terrace deposits yielded good gold values in the past.

At ***Redding*** we meet I-5, and the Upper Sacramento River. Some 5 miles north of Redding and west of I-5, is *Old Diggings*, a big hydraulic placer area. Check the higher bench gravels.

Continuing south on I-5 to Cottonwood, where the Cottonwood Creek empties into the Sacramento River. Do some pannings in Crow, Dry, Antelope and Roaring River Creeks.

Other areas of interest in Shasta County are ***Dog Creek***, west of Castilla in the northwestern area and ***Harrison Gulch***, on the Middle Fork of Cottonwood Creek just off A-16 from Platina.

Campgrounds: ***Redding*** — Bear Mountain RV Resort — all year — 97 sites — private — (916)275-4728
KOA — open all year — 119 sites — (916) 246-0101.
Platina — Basin Gulch — May 20 to November 1 — 15 sites — National Forests — (916) 352-4211.

Motels: ***Redding*** — Ponderosa Inn (Best Western) — 70 units — (916) 241-6300
Super 8 — 80 units — (916) 221-8881.

Anderson — Knights Inn (Best Western) — 40 units — Restaurant adjacent — (916) 365-2753.

* * *

In the southern part of the State we find the desert areas and the lower ranges (Transverse and Peninsular). Some seven counties occupy these geomorphic provinces while two more counties are contained within the Nevadian Basin and Range topography.

The two counties in the Mohave Desert province are Imperial, adjacent to Arizona and Mexico, and the large county of San Bernardino which adjoins Nevada and Arizona.

Imperial County.

Entering California at Winterhaven from Yuma, Arizona, a dirt road leads north for 18 miles to the Picocho Recreation Area on the Colorado River. The washes of the ***Picocho Mountains*** have run gold values in dry washings of the past. The deposits are reportedly shallow and discontinuous.

At ***Potholes***, some 10 miles south of Picocho near the Laguna Dam, some $2 million in dry washing was recovered. The area has rough terrain, little rainfall and erratic gold value distribution.

Going west from Winterhaven along I-8, we turn north at Felicity (13 miles) on to county road S-34. Some 5 miles north, the village of Ogilby is in the foothills of the Cargo Muchaco mountains. Try dry washing the local gulches, particularly Jackson gulch. Continuing north we pick up highway 78 some 10 miles northeast of Glamis. The Chocolate mountains southwest from here to Glamis are closed to the public because of naval and army gunnery practice. Check out the dry washes between here and Midway Wells to the north and Glamis to the south. Incidentally, the foothill washes of these mountains east of Niland at the Peg Leg Well ran extremely high grade for a prospector in the late thirties. Continue on highway 78 west to Brawley.

Superstition Hills. Located some 23 miles west of Brawley and just southwest of the intersection of highways 78 and 86. Parts of this area are closed by the military to the public. The dry washes have gold particles coated with a black oxide covering. There are small rich pockets reported here.

Campgrounds: ***Winterhaven*** — Pilot Knob RV Park — all year — 105 suites — Private —(619) 572-5232.

Picocho State Recreation Area — all year — 50 sites — no phone.

El Centro — Desert Trails RV Park — all year — 365 sites — Private — (619) 352-7275.

El Centro KOA — open all year — 181 sites — Private — (619) 353-1051.

Motels: ***Yuma,*** *Arizona* — Desert Grove Motel — 24 units — kitchens — (602)344-1921

Yuma Cabana Motel — 63 units — kitchens — (602) 783-8311.

Brawley, *California* — Town House Lodge — 39 units — (619) 344-5120.

* * *

San Bernardino.

The desert area of this large county takes up all but the southwestern corner. This portion is contained within the Transverse and Peninsular Range belt.

Starting our expedition at ***Twentynine Palms*** on highway 62. Some early placering was done in the cemented gravels of the dry washes north of this town in the Bullion Mountains. Unfortunately sections of this mountain range are closed off by the Marine Corps. Inquire before going too deep into the mountains. Some of the washes in the various hills and mountain ranges south of the town show color and are worthy of investigation.

Figure C-4: Early California Miners

Some 22 miles east of Twentynine Palms, county road 247 heads toward Barstow. At ***Lucerne Valley***, roads lead northeast into the Ord Mountains. Several of the gulches and washes, including Camp Rock, have good placer possibilities.

Returning to Lucerne Valley, head south on highway 18 to Big Bear Lake. We are now entering the San Bernardino Mountains. The slopes north of ***Big Bear Lake*** (Holcomb Valley) have been placered in the past with satisfying results. East of ***Baldwin Lake***, in such places as Rattlesnake Gulch, Little Horse Thief Canyon and Arrastre Creek placering has been carried on. Travelling further west, along #38 and up #15, to ***Lytle Creek***, 8 miles north of San Bernardino, we enter the San Gabriel Mountains. The creek issuing from the canyon is old placering ground.Try a few pans here. Private property here.

It should be noted that the western San Gabriel Mountains, behind Los Angeles, have seen a great deal of placering in the old days. Buildings plus present day regulations rule against placering. We now continue north on I-15 to Barstow.

Grapevine. This area is located some 14 miles north of Barstow in the Paradise mountains. Some good dry placer washes are located here. To the west , ***Coolgardie*** lies some 6 miles northeast of Harper Lake, between Paradise and the Black Mountains. Gravel county roads from highway 58 lead north into this desert valley area. This is a dry washer area where results have been good in the past.

Continuing on by #58 and #395 to ***Randsburg***, some 60 miles from Barstow, numerous small gold mines have been worked in the Rand Mountains just behind the town. The dry washes in these mountains and also in the El Paso Mountains, 15 miles west, have been productive.

It should be stated here that a good placering location is at ***Piru***, in Ventura county, come 10 miles west on highway 126, off I-5. The placer deposits are in the upper part of Piru Creek, particularly at the junction with Lockwood Creek. Check the terrace deposits north of the creek.

We now head north towards the famous Sierra Nevada Mountains stopping at several Basin and Range deposits en route.

Campgrounds:

Twentynine Palms — 29 Palms RV Resort — open all year — 196 sites — Private — (619) 367-3320

Big Bear Lake — Coldbrook — May 15 to Nov. 15 — 36 sites — National Forest — (714) 866-3437.

Victorville — Golden Pond RV Park — open all year — 88 sites — Private — (619) 246-5879.

Victorville KOA — open all year — 136 sites — Private — (619) 245-6867.

Barstow — Barstow KOA — open all year — 72 sites — Private — (619) 254-2311.

Owl Canyon — open all year — 31 sites — Bureau of Land Management — (619) 256-3591.

Piru — Blue Point — open all year — 42 sites — National Forest — (805) 646-4348.

Motels: ***Twentynine Palms*** — Gardens Motel (Best Western) — 71 units — (619) 367-9141.

Desert Inn — Senior discount — 125 units — restaurant — (619) 367-2833.

Running Springs — Cloud 9 Lodge — 7 kitchen cottages — (714) 867-2400.

Victorville — Scottish Inns — Senior discount — 21 units — (619) 243-5858.

* * *

Inyo and Mono Counties.

These two counties are located in east-central California, flush against the Nevada border. They are part of the Basin and Range province which lies just east of the Sierra Nevadas.

Wildrose is 25 miles from Randsburg, north on #178 in Inyo county. Located in the Panamint Mountains, numerous dry washes have run small, modest grade but discontinuous deposits.

Via #178 and #395, north on #395 to Independence. ***Tibbetts*** is located just east of the highway ten miles further north. Placer deposits were worked by dry methods in the old days and during the depression years at Mazourka Canyon.

From Independence north to Benton on I-6 is 78 miles. The ***White Mountains*** area in Mono county, some 10 miles southeast of Benton has seen a lot of stream placering along the canyons of the western edge of the range. It might be well to pan a few of these streams.

Cross over highway 120 (if in the summer) to ***Jordan***, a few miles north of Mono Lake on #395. This is one of the few placer areas known on the east flank of the Sierra Nevadas. The auriferous gravels eroded from the Sierras form poorly defined channels of variable thickness and erratic gold values. Several old diggings (Mono and Dogtown Diggings) are located in this district.

From Mono Lake up to Bridgeport and on to Patterson, 15 miles to the northwest in the Sweetwater Mountains. Early canyons of interest were Silverado and Fryingpan Canyons. The area has seen a lot of production in the late 1800's.

Now we travel into the most prolific gold placer producer of California — for that matter, the southwest — the Sierra Nevada Mountains.

Campgrounds: ***Wildrose*** — Wildrose RV — open all year — 20 sites — National Parks Service — (619) 786-2331.

Bishop (numerous sites) — East Fork — open May 1 to Nov. 1 — 133 sites — National Forests — (619) 873-4207.

Pleasant Valley — open all year — 200 sites — County — (619)878-2411 Ext.2272

Bridgeport (numerous sites) Honeymoon — open April 20 to Oct. 5 — 47 sites — National Forest —(619) 932-7070.

Motels: ***Bridgeport*** — Silver Maple Inn — 18 units — restaurant close by — (619) 932-7383.

Bishop — El Rancho Motel — 16 units — 3 kitchen units — (619) 872-9251.

We now travel into the most interesting and most prolific gold producing area in the United States — the Sierra Nevada Mountains. As of 1965, the dollar values of gold production from the 21 counties making up this area totalled $2,000 million. This is in contrast to $242 million from the Klamath

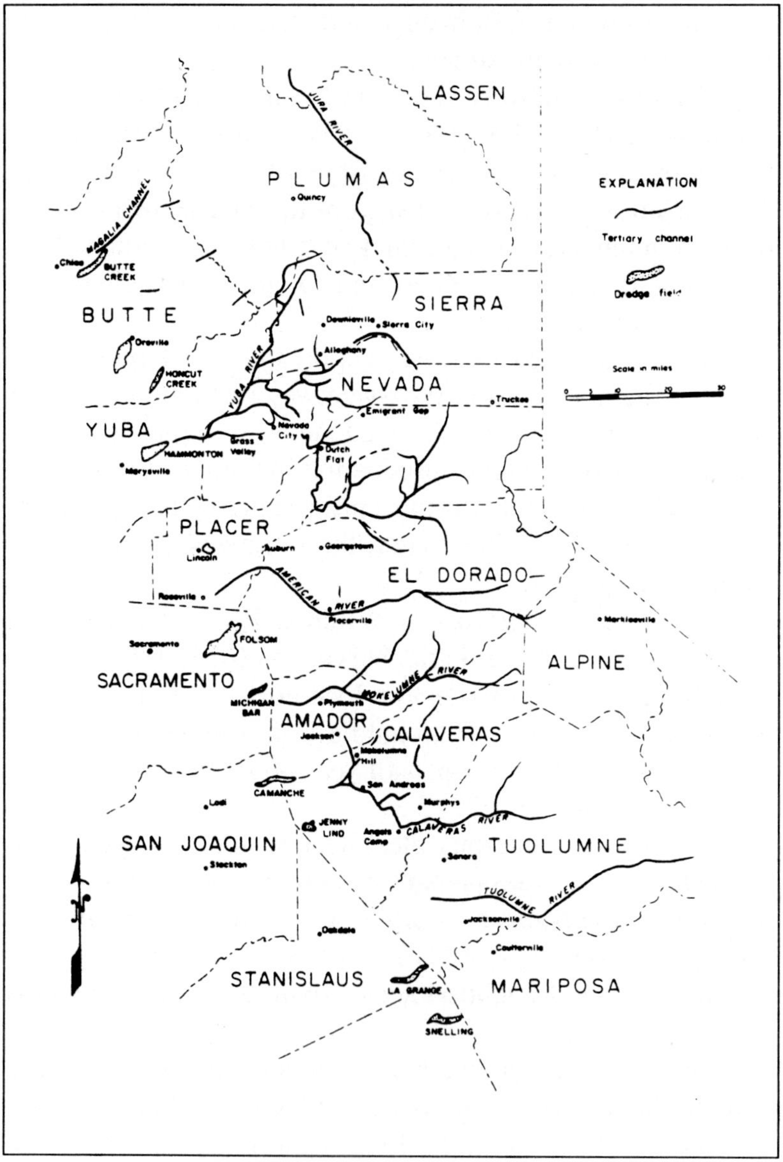

Figure C-5: Sierra Nevadas

Mountains area and $44 million from the Desert province and $52 million from the two counties in the Basin and Range province.

Physiographically the range extends over 450 miles on a north-south trend, is 50 to 80 miles wide, has a long gentle western slope and a high, steep eastern escarpment.

It is these mountains that acted as hosts to the mass hysteria that was termed "gold fever". The spotting of small gold nuggets at Sutters Mill in January of 1848 precipitated the onrush of gold seekers into California, originating the Great Gold Rush of 1849. Eventually the placer miners located the "Mother Lode" system of lode mines. The stampede continued in full swing. The flood of miners quickly exhausted the rich surface placers in the riverbeds and soon extended to the flat ridgetops where the Tertiary high gravels were found and prospected. The miners worked these gravels by two methods. If exposed as high gravel banks they were "hydraulicked" by subjecting them to jets of high pressure water. The material dislodged was run through giant sluice boxes and the discharge was emptied into present day streams. Where hydraulicking was impossible for physical or economical reasons, the miners "drift mined" by a series of horizontal,or vertical, passageways to the gold-bearing gravels at the base of the channel.

These Tertiary deposits took on more significance with the exhaustion of the surface deposits. Geologists have concluded that three major Tertiary rivers — Yuba, American and Mokelumne — and four minor Tertiary streams — Calaveras, Tuolumne, Feather and Magalia — have contributed to the high level Tertiary gravels of today. See Figure C-5. A report on these Tertiary gravels published in 1968 estimated reserves of these gravels to total 3 to 4 billion cubic yards with an average grade of 0.007 ounces ($2.50) per cubic yard (gold $350 per ounce). Some 600 to 800 million cubic yards within the lower sections of these gravels were estimated at an average grade of 0.029 ounces ($10) per cubic yard. These Tertiary deposits are often hidden under lava cappings, or later gravel beds. Refer to Chapter 3.

In examining the placer possibilities of the Sierra Nevadas, we will go through each individual county involved in the Rush, starting at the most southern,Kern, and working north to the final county, Butte. It should be noted that the 5 counties which are considered to hold the "Mother Lode" underground deposits are - El Dorado, Amador, Calaveras, Tuolumne and Mariposa.

Kern. In this, the most southern of the Sierra Nevada counties, the mountain range is winding down before giving way to the Mohave Desert physiography.

Using Bakersfield as the starting point, we travel northeast on highway 178 along the **Kern River.** This was a well placered river in the old days, particularly from 15 miles south of Hot Springs through to Lake Isabella. At Hobo Hot Springs, **Clear Creek** empties into the Kern. Check it out. Similarly, just north of Bodfish, **Erskine Creek**, an early placer stream, joins the Kern. Both creeks come out of the Pirete Mountains, a good placering location. At Lake Isabella, travelling back (west) into the **Greenhouse Mountains** gives opportunity to do panning at the various creeks, particularly Greenhorn Creek, Fremont Creek, Bradshaw Creek and Black Gulch Creek. Continuing on highway 155 from Lake Isabella, a county road going southwest at Glennville runs by **Mannot Creek**, a distance of 12 miles. Gold has been reported in this creek.

Continuing from Bakersfield north on Highway 99 we enter Fresno County at Kingsburg 90 miles north. On through to Fresno (10 miles).

At Fresno, take highway 180 east. At Dunlop (30 miles) **Mill Creek** crosses on its way to Kings River. Rich surface placers were discovered here in the Rush. Some 12 miles further east Mill Flat Creek flows south across the roadway. An 8 mile road following the creek leads to **Sampson Flat**, an early placer find. Returning to Centerville on 180, travel northeast towards Pine Flat Reservoir. At Piedra, the creeks at **Sycamore Flat**, just to the north, have run colors in the past. Check Hughes Creek. Continuing northeast on this county road for some 10 miles beyond Trimmer we enter the **Big Creek** area. Good panning here. Cross over at Pine Ridge to Auberry on 168. **Temperance Flat**, which saw active placer-mining in the old days, is on the south side of Millerton Lake. Continuing around the south end of the Lake, we enter **Friant**. Here large gravel plants extract gold from the river gravels and small terrace deposits alongside the river.

Campgrounds: ***Fresno***

Millerton Lake State Recreational Area — open all year — 131 sites — (209) 822-2332.

Big Creek

West Kaiser — June 15 to Nov. 1 — 10 sites — RV limit: 22' — National Forest — (209) 841-3311.

Centerville

Pine Flat Lake — open all year — 73 sites — RV limit: 20' — Corps of Engineers — (209) 787-2589.

Motels: ***Fresno***

(numerous) Tradewinds (Best Western) — 110 units — senior discount — (209) 237-1881.

Hill House Vagabond Inn — 98 units — coffee shop — (209) 268-6211.

Econo Lodge — 56 units — (209) 442-1082

From Fresno we travel north on 41 and enter <u>Madera County</u> at Pinedale. Continuing northeast on this scenic highway we enter an extensive gold placering area at **Coarsegold**. It is at this location that Highway 49 — Path of the '49ers — begins. A good gold panning section extends northwest from here for some 8 miles to **Great Gulch** and continues southeast for an additional 10 miles to a ghost town called **Fine Gold**. On the north side of Millerton Lake, good placering existed at **Hildreth**, just south of O'Neals. Continuing north on Highway 99, check out the river gravels on the **Fresno** and **Chowchilla** rivers.

Campgrounds: ***Oakhurst***

4 National Forests operations —- all with 12 sites — open May 21 - Nov. 15 — (209) 683-4665.

Chowchilla

Eastman Lake — 79 sites — open all year — Operating Engineers — (209) 689-3255.

Motels: ***Madera***

Valley Inn (Best Western) — 93 units — coffee shop — (209) 673-5164.

Oakhurst

Yosemite Gateway Inn (Best Western) — 118 units — (209) 683-2378.

Going north on 99 we enter Merced County. Merced, like Stanislaus, San Joaquin and Sacramento counties, is in the western foothills of the Sierra Nevadas. Because of this location — being part of the Great Valley — these counties were the recipients of the great outpourings of the ancient Tertiary rivers of the Sierra Nevadas into the marine waters which filled the valley. The present day rivers, in certain instances, flood their plains in these counties as they emerge from the hills. As a consequence the counties have large placer dredge areas where the gold bearing gravels of the recent and ancient rivers spread into the valley. Check out the surface gravels in the vicinity of these dredge locations but be careful of farming developments.

In Merced, **Snelling** is the principal dredging field. It is located on the Merced River, 17 miles northeast of Merced on state highway 59 . The dredge field is nine miles long by one mile wide with gravels varying from 20 to 35 feet in depth. Dredging of this field is estimated to have produced some $17 million in fine gold. Platinum is also present.

In Stanislaus County, adjoining to the north, the Tuolumne River has given rise to a similar situation at **La Grange**, 11 miles north of Snelling on highway 132. The gravels are estimated to have yielded in excess of $13 million in gold. At **Knight's Ferry**, 10 miles east of Oakdale on highway 120, considerable placer mining of the river gravels was undertaken by the Forty-Niners and later Chinese miners. Try a few pans if possible.

In the next northerly county, San Joaquin, the dredging field is located east of **Clements,** on highway 88. This area is presently part of the **Camanche** Reservoir. At one time the huge field extended 12 miles back up the Mokelumne River. Some $10 million in gold is reported to have been recovered.

In Sacramento County lying north of San Joaquin, there are two large placer dredge fields. **Michigan Bar** is located on the Consumnes River some 20 miles east of Sacramento where highway 16 crosses the river, in the vicinity of Sloughhouse. Total production has been estimated at 1 3/4 million ounces. Off highway 50 at **Folsom**, the present day American River has been dredged downcurrent for some 10 miles. This was the largest and richest dredged section in California, however large areas of the field presently host industrial and housing tracts. Total output was estimated at $125 million.

Several other large dredge fields exist in Placer, Yuba and Butte counties. We will discuss these as we proceed.

Figure C-6: Early California Miners

There are numerous campgrounds in the counties already mentioned including:

Merced: ***Chowchilla***

Eastman Lake — open all year — 79 sites — Operating Engineers — (209) 689-3255.

Stanislaus: ***La Grange***

Barret Cove — open all year — 275 sites — District — (209) 378-2711.

San Joaquin: ***Lode***

Tower Park — open all year — 402 sites — Private — (209) 369-1041.

Sacramento: ***Folsom***

Folsom Lake — open all year — 68 sites — State — (916) 988-0205.

Motels: ***Merced***

Best Western Inn — senior discount — 42 units — (209) 723-2163.

Turlock

Almond Tree Inn — 92 units — (209) 668-3400.

Stockton

Motel Orleans — 70 units — senior discount — (209)931-9341

Sacramento

(numerous) Sandman Hotel (Best Western) — senior discount — 116 units — (916) 443-6515.

Returning now to the most southern of the "Mother Lode Counties" — Mariposa. The Mother Lode deposit system extends over a 120 mile distance through 5 counties; is composed of linked (in echelon) gold-quartz veins and varies from a 70 mile width at the north end (Butte-Plumas) to one mile in the south (Mariposa). The more than 40 lode mines that operated in this belt since 1850 have yielded greater than $300 million in gold from veins exceeding 6000 feet in depth. The discovery of these lode mines was the direct follow-up of placer exploration. It is estimated that some $400 million of gold was extracted from the placer deposits within the 5 counties. In addition four of the Tertiary rivers traversing these 5 counties left buried remnants behind. However, Mariposa was not as lucky as the other 4 counties in this respect.

At **Mormon Bar** on highway 49, early placering was done on Mariposa Creek. Some 75,000 ounces of gold was reported from creeks in this area. At Mariposa, travelling up highway 140 towards Yosemite Village we parallel Merced River which has yielded colors. A few miles beyond Briceburg , travel up the South Fork to **Hite Cove**. Check the creeks entering the South Fork. Back to highway 49. At **Mt. Bullion** some 5 miles north of Mariposa, creeks like Agua Fria, issuing out of the Guadalope Mountains should be panned. Further north a county road leads off to McClure Lake Recreation Area leading through **Hunter Valley**. Some of the creeks entering the lake should be examined. Be careful of private property here. At **Coulterville** on highway 49, the Forty-Niners did extensive placering. A road east from here leads to **Kinsley**, 5 miles distant. Extensive placer operations took place at Bull Creek, Gentry Gulch and other creeks entering the North Fork of the Merced River.

Travelling north on 49 we enter Tuolumne County with its Tertiary benches of the ancient Tuolumne River.

At the junction of 49 and 120 we head east towards Yosemite on 120 and pass through **Big Oak Flat**, a few miles beyond. At Big Oak and Deer Flat, the high grade gravels produced over $25 million in gold. Check whatever streams you encounter. A further 12 miles to Buck Meadows where the Tertiary gravels at Dorseys and Smith Station in the **Gravel Range** yielded good results. Returning to highway 49, where the highway crosses the Tuolumne River at **Jacksonville**, high grade gravels placered many ounces of gold. Ten miles further upstream on the **Tuolumne River** shallow gravel deposits were mined in the original Rush. At **Chinese Camp**, a few miles further up the highway, the gulches show the early placer efforts which won some $2.5 million in gold flakes from the Tertiary quartzitic gravels. Check Woods Creek. At **Jamestown**, 7 miles along, small shaft headframes of the Mother Lode system spot the area. Some Tertiary gravel deposits underlie volcanic capping in this vicinity. At **Sonora**, a few miles further, the rich early day placer deposits of Sonora and Shaws Flat were found in deep crevices and potholes in the limestone formations of the area. Some 8 miles north in the Columbia State Historical Park is the **Columbia Diggings**, a very famous placer-mining district. Estimates of production vary from $87 to $150 million. It is a preserved Tertiary valley with rich potholes in the limestones. One large nugget from here weighed over 600 ounces while several exceeded 300 ounces.

At Melones, we enter Calaveras County, with its multitude of Mother Lode mines and Forty-Niner diggings plus Tertiary showings of the ancient Calaveras River.

At **Angels Camp**, a few miles up the highway we encounter one of the most famous mining camps of the California Gold Rush. It is both a lode and placer site. Several miles north two famous drift mines, the Altaville and Calaveras Central, mined (Altaville still does) the Tertiary Central Channel of the ancestral Calaveras River. Some 5 miles east at Vallecito, the channel outcrops and two tributary channel, Murphy's Gulch and Cataract, join the main channel. Intensive placering went on in this area during the Rush and Depression years. The quartzitic gravels which carried coarse gold were often overlain by volcanic cover and/or by later gravels. A good area to check out! More than likely very little land will be available for location. This Tertiary Channel extends east up highway 4 to **Murphys** while north from here at **Sheep Ranch**, on San Antonio Creek, we encounter what is known as the Fort Mountain channel.

Continuing north on highway 49, a few miles south of San Andreas we run across two remnants of the Tertiary Fort Mountain Channel, one at **Calaveritas**, on Calaveritas Creek, and further north another on O'Neils Creek. At **San Andreas** the main Central Hill Channel continues northwest. The Fort Mountain Channel joins the Central Hill between Calaveritas and San Andreas. Is this getting confusing? Remember whereas today we call the different sections of a river by 'North Fork' or 'South Fork', the older Tertiary river splits are each called by a different channel name.

Figure C-7: Panning in the North

Some 18 miles west of San Andreas, just off highway 26, **Jenny Lind** has been the locale of intensive placering initially by hand methods, then later by hydraulic and dredge. The gravels are flood plains of the present Calaveras River. Seven miles north of San Andreas on 49 is **Mokelumne Hill**, a very famous placer area during the Rush period. Eight distinct Tertiary channels have been mined in different placer approaches. Some of the gravels were fabulous! You might not be able to do any panning here but a visit to this historical site is well worthwhile. **Railroad Flat**, 15 miles east of Mokelumne

Hill, just off highway 26 on the South Fork of the present-day Mokelumne River, is on the Tertiary Fort Mountain Channel. This could be an interesting area to investigate.

We continue on highway 49 into Amador County. A 12 mile long belt of the Mother Lode gold mineralization runs through this county from **Jackson to Plymouth**. This belt was one of the more important gold-mining districts in the nation. Here 15 lode mines produced in excess of 8 million ounces of gold! Several Tertiary channels of the ancient Mokelumne River run through this county including exposures at **Pine Grove,** then at **Volcano**, just off highway 88 from Pine Grove, and further northeast at **White Oak Flat**. Continuing on highway 49 to Drytown where some 6 miles downstream on Dry Creek from Drytown, and just off highway 124, is **Irish Hill**. Tertiary gravels are located in this vicinity. The extension of these gravels outcrops at **Fiddletown** just east of Plymouth. Try to catch the base of these Tertiary gravels as this is where most of the gold is resting.

Campgrounds in the last 4 counties are:

Mariposa County

Midpines — open all year — 86 sites — reserve deposit — KOA — (209) 966-2201.

Coulterville —RV Park - open all year-31 sites - private - (209)878-3988

Tuolumne County

Groveland — 6 locations run by National Forest — from 10 to 46 sites — open from April - November — (209) 962-7825.

Columbia — open all year — 85 sites — reserve deposit — private — (209) 532-9539.

Calaveras County

Valley Springs — open all year — 121 sites — Operating Engineers — (209) 772-1343.

Amador County

Plymouth — open all year — 329 sites — reserve deposit — private — (209) 245-6981.

No motels are stated as there are plenty along this scenic route. Most are involved with a chain - Super 8, Best Western, etc.

Continuing along the Path of the '49ers we enter El Dorado county, which has remnants of the ancient American and Mokelumne Rivers within its domain. At **Placerville**, an extensive placer and lode area, we pick up Tertiary remnants of the old American River. This remnant extends southeast for 5 miles to **Newtown** on Weber Creek and north through **Coloma** to **Pilot Hill**. It was here at Pilot Hill that a gold-quartz boulder containing some 400 ounces of gold was dug out. Incidentally, Coloma is the location of the historic find of gold in Sutter's Mill. It would be interesting to check some of the hydraulic tailings left behind, say at Placerville's **Texas Hill**, **Negro Hill**, and **Sacramento Hill** and at Newtown's **Camino** and **Pleasant Valley** locations. Most of this ground is privately owned. Some 25 miles east of Placerville, a Tertiary tributary of the Mokelumne River passes south through **Grizzly Flat** to **Indian Diggings** on the way to joining the main Tertiary channel in Amador County. Other isolated Tertiary occurrences are at **Fairplay** which displayed rich benches (near Somerset on E16), **Georgetown** off 49 on #193 and **Volcanoville**, a few miles north of Georgetown. At Greenwood, just west of Georgetown, skin divers probe the present day gravels of the Middle Fork of the American River.

Following highway 49 north into Placer County we find the name is well applied. The early Tertiary channels of the American River appear quite frequently and are geologically confusing as to their direction. There have been as many diversions in the ancient river as there are in the present day river. Witness the number of "forks" of this river, the Yuba (most confusing) and the Feather, plus their numerous tributaries. The early channels are, and have been, worked by the drift mine approach. This is of no help to the RV panner. Placer County has an unusually large number of drift mines, some as deep as 400 feet to bedrock.

At Auburn, Highway 49 intersects the east-west Interstate 80. This speedway closely parallels the main Tertiary Channel of the American River. Exposures, which were hydraulically worked or drift mined, are at **Rochlin** (14 miles S.W. of Auburn), **Forest Hill** (12 miles N.E. of Auburn), **Iowa Hill** (just off I-80), **Gold River** (13 miles north of Forest Hill) and **Michigan Bluff** (6 miles east of Iowa Hill). Some surface mining (panning) is available on the American and Bear River at **Colfax** (I-80); at **Rocklin** (I-80) on Pleasant Grove Creek (also Tertiary here); **Lincoln** (Highway 65) along Auburn and Doty Ravines, and **Wheatland** (10 miles north of Lincoln on 65), plus some of the creeks and ravines of the Bear river.

Carrying on north from Auburn on Highway 49 we enter Nevada County, another placer rich area with heavy hydraulic-worked sections. The middle fork of the Yuba divides Nevada county from Yuba on the north. The south fork of the Yuba (both ancient and present-day) are contained within Nevada County. Highway 49 passes through **Grass Valley**, the locale of a large number of famous lode gold mines including the Empire (which closed in 1957), the Idaho and the North Star. At **Nevada City**, 3 miles further north , 4 tributary channels of the ancient Yuba River were home to more than 20 deep drift mines. However the major channel of the Tertiary Yuba is picked up at **Englebright Lake** on 49 some 8 miles north of Nevada City. It roughly parallels the present day course of the middle fork of the Yuba save for being several miles to the south. It continues northeastward through the communities of **North San Juan**, **Badger Hill**,

North Columbia and **North Bloomfield** then southeast to **Washington**. These are important "diggings" located along this channel which resulted from the hydraulic mining period of 1853 to 1884 at which time hydraulic mining was legally curtailed in the Sierra Nevadas. The **Malakoff** hydraulic mine site ("diggings") at North Bloomfield is over 7000 feet long, 3000 feet wide and 600 feet deep. The Chinese carried on small-scale placer mining on the hydraulic tailings in these counties from 1890 to well into the 1900's. There is little that the active RV miner can do with these hydraulic tailings, or the Tertiary channel for that matter, except study and be impressed by them. If you are lucky enough to find a bench with Tertiary gravels resting on bedrock, or gravels overlain by volcanic lava, it would be worthwhile to run some pans. Most of these channels have been staked out. The writer visited a workings some six miles east of Washington where at a canyon the bottom gravels of the present-day South Fork of the Yuba were being exploited by a drag line method. A huge scraper was dragged along the bed of the river pulling the gravels to a collection point. A front end loader delivered the gravels to a trommel with a three sluice box set-up. They were extracting several ounces of gold per shift.

Several tributary Tertiary channels blend with the main Yuba one in this vicinity. One highly investigated channel runs north from **Scotts Flat** just off Highway 20, 7 miles east of Nevada City, cuts north across the present day South Fork of the Yuba at a place called **Blue Tent** and joins the main channel at **North Columbia**.

Adjoining Placer lie the counties of Yuba on the west and Sierra on the north. Going west on I-20 from Grass Valley, we enter <u>Yuba County</u> at **Smartsville**, 15 miles west. Here the Main Channel of the Tertiary Yuba River enters from the Englebright Lake area. Better than $6 gold was mined from this channel during hydraulic action. Continuing on to Hammonton, 10 miles further west on I-20 we enter a large dredge field that operated up to 1968. This area is on the lower Yuba River and originated from flood conditions of the river and hydraulic tailings emptied into the river. During a 70 year dredge period some 235 million yards of gravel were treated (better than 9000 yards per day) yielding just over 5 million ounces of gold (0.02 ounces gold per cubic yard).

Returning to Grass Valley we head north on highway 49 into Sierra County. Exiting at North San Juan we encounter the Tertiary Main Channel of the North Fork of the Yuba River. See figure C-5. This channel is often referred to as the La Porte Channel. Here at North San Juan it joins the Middle Fork of the Yuba previously referred to. The channel indirectly parallels the present south channel of the Feather River some 5-10 miles to the east, as it carries northeast through **Comptonville**, in Yuba County, **Indian Hill**, **Brandy City** and **Poverty Hill** to **La Porte** in Plumas County. Here a branch termed the Port Wine channel enters from **Gibsonville**. Continuing on highway 49 to **Downieville** we encounter a part of the present Yuba River system where skin diving for gold in the bottom gravels is permitted with proper safety precautions. The Yuba River and its smaller streams in this area offer extensive river and terrace gravel for prospecting. At **Alleghany**, 10 miles south by road, a tributary Tertiary channel, called Forest Channel, enters from **American Hill** and then strikes south to join the Middle Fork Tertiary Yuba close to the Malakoff diggings in Nevada County. The creeks around Alleghany attract many skin divers chasing the gold gravels. Highway 49 ends in the high Sierras at Vinton on US 70 in Plumas County.

The two most northern counties in the Sierras — Butte and Plumas — have good representation in the placer area. Both counties host the Feather River with its three forks. Butte on the west is along the foothills while Plumas nestles back into the higher ground.

Highway 70 runs in a rough east-west direction through Plumas and ends at Oroville, a main supply town, on highways 149 and 99 in Butte county. Highway 89 runs in a north-south

Figure C-9: Examining a monument

bearing through Plumas with no placer deposits being located west of highways 149 and 99 in Butte.

Heading west on highway 70 from Vinton, we follow the Middle Fork of the Feather River downstream and enter a lode and placer area at **Johnsville**, 5 miles west of Blairsden. This is ski country in the high Sierras and is contained in a State Park. Check some of the creeks in this area. At Quincy, 25 miles west, we enter **American** and **Thompson Valleys**, both of which are underlain by Recent and Pleistocene alluvium gravels which are gold-bearing in places. Following a county road west from Quincy along a tributary creek, **Meadow Valley** 8 miles upstream has Tertiary gravel patches (Spanish Ranch) plus auriferous Pleistocene lake gravels. On highway 70 at **Rich Bar** the North Fork of the Feather River combines with several tributaries and turns to flow south. At this point the river executes a series of sharp bends resulting in the formation of wide gravel bars which have been gold-rich in the past.

We could have avoided the "big bend" in route 70 by continuing on from Johnsville by county road to **La Porte**. Prior to La Porte at a point some 20 miles from Johnsville, where the South and Middle Fork of the Feather River meet is an old hydraulic area called Sawpit Flat. Present day placering is carried on here at Monitor Flat while skin divers check out the local river and creek gravels. The Tertiary showings here form part of the main La Porte channel. La Porte, 20 miles from Johnsville, is one of the greater placer-mining districts in the state. The main Tertiary channel of the North Fork of the Yuba River, (La Porte channel) extends northeast to Gibsonville and south to Poverty Hill, both in Sierra county. In Chapter 6, I mentioned examining a drift mine near here which sank 250 feet to bedrock before drifting on rich ore in the La Porte Channel. Two other notable placers in this county are **Light's Canyon**, in the northeast corner and **Mooreville Ridge**, in the southwest section. Both locations have exposed Tertiary beds which have been mined in the past by hydraulic methods. At the latter place, 8 miles south of La Porte, placering by the skin diving approach is popular.

We now enter the last of our northern Sierra Nevada counties — Butte. This county has high gold production mainly from its dredging operations and drift mines.

Figure C-10: Duke's Test Plant

If we enter Butte from the east side on highway 70, we pass over Lake Oroville some 14 miles northeast of Oroville. A few miles west of this huge reservoir we encounter 2 areas situated on the same Tertiary channel — **Cherokee** and **Morris Ravine**. This channel has been extensively hydraulically operated in the past. Some creeks in the area might be worth investigating. Just south of Cherokee is highway 191 going north to to Sterling City. A few miles west of Paradise on this highway is **Butte Creek**, another extensive Tertiary Channel which extends south for 4 miles and north to **Magalia**, a distance of 9 miles. This main Magalia Channel had large stream and bench gravels and due to its intersection at Magalia with several other channels, the gold was coarse indicating short travel distance. In addition, small diamonds and platinum minerals were common here. Some 5 miles south on this channel, shore gravels where the ancient river emptied into a lake were identified. A good amount of dredging took place on the Magalia Channel. On highway 191 some 10 miles north of Sterling City is **Kimshew**. Located on the West Fork of the Feather River it has Tertiary and Recent gravels available.

Where 70 joins 99 is **Oroville**, a huge dredge field. The Yuba and Feather Rivers emptied into the Ione Sea in this vicinity. The dredge area is one mile by nine miles long and is estimated to have yielded close to two million ounces of gold.

Entering Butte County on the La Porte Road (CR-511) from Blairsden we encounter **Clipper Mills** 14 miles south of La Port, **Forbestown** 5 miles further,**Bangor** 16 miles along, and **Honcut** an additional 9 miles south, all large placer dredge fields. The latter location is thought to be a Tertiary delta deposit of the ancient Yuba River. A 14 pound nugget was found in these diggings.

Campgrounds: Butte County

Sterling City

2 locations — Total 33 sites — open May 25 - Nov. 1 — National Forest — (916) 258-2141.

Oroville

211 sites — open all year — state operated —(916) 538-2200.

Plumas County

La Porte

2 locations — total 160 sites — open June 15- Oct. 1 — National Forest — (916) 675-2462.

Sierra County

Downieville

Union Flat — 16 sites — open May 1 - Oct. 1 — National Forest — (916) 288-3231.

Yuba County

Marysville

Collins Lake — 154 sites — open all year — reserve deposit — private — (916) 692-1600.

Challenge

2 locations — 29 sites — open April 1- December 1 — National Forest — (916) 675-2462.

Nevada

Nevada City

2 locations — 34 sites — open June 15- Oct. 1 — National Forest — (916) 265-4536.

Malakoff Diggings

30 sites — open all year — State Historical Park — (916) 265-2740

One final word before we leave California. The Sierra Nevada area has been well populated and many of the old placer areas are held by private interests. If you find anything of interest on private property, you might be able to strike a deal with the owner. Also don't be dismayed or awed by the extent and size of the Tertiary channels. Instead check for more recent deposits in small streams and creeks in these vicinities. Creeks percolating through the old tailings from the hydraulic or dredge operations could have picked up some fragmental gold and carried it away. Remember not everything was recovered by the old-timers but they did get the richest pickings!

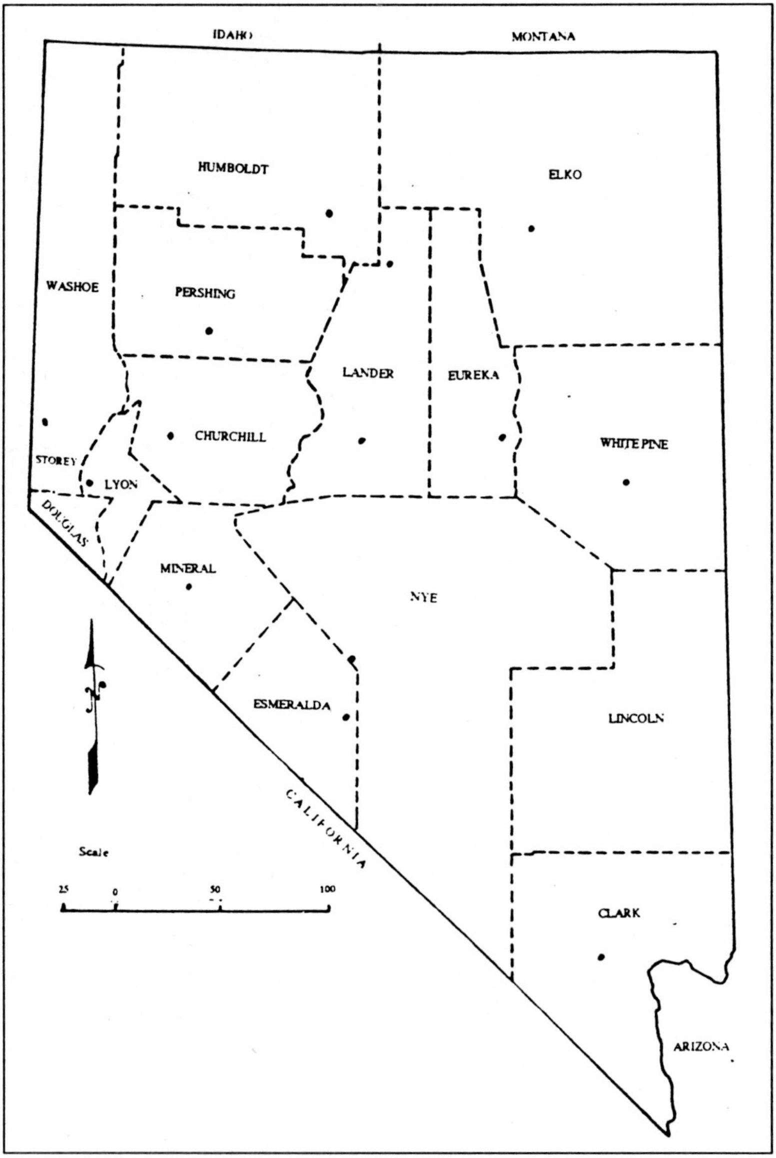

Figure N-1: Nevada

NEVADA

The seventh largest State in the Union with one of the smallest populations (1.1 million). Built on mining, Nevada today ranks sixth among the states in the annual production of gold. Although its fame and early settlement was based on silver, gold has in the last half century surpassed silver.

Historians record incursions into the hot deserts of Nevada by Spanish priests in 1776 followed by Hudson's Bay Company trappers in 1820. Captain Freemont led expeditions into the state in 1843 - 45 but it was the Mormons who established in 1850 permanent residency first at Genoa (18 miles south of Carson City) and then in 1855 at another mission, eventually to be named Las Vegas.

The discovery of placer gold at Gold Canyon in 1850 initiated interest in the state. However, it was the realization of the importance of the Comstock Lode in 1859 which provided Nevada with one of the richest concentrations of gold and silver in the United States.

This 3 mile length of ore zone supplied in excess of $400 million in gold-silver ore since its discovery. It was the output from the Comstock Lode which financed the Union's effort during the Civil War.

Nevada received statehood in 1864, the same year that Samuel Clements (Mark Twain) left Virginia City. In 1931 Nevada legalized gambling thus making tourism its number one industry. Mining to this day closely follows in the number two spot. A careful husbanding of the water resources has assisted in the irrigation of previous desert land along the western sections of the state and has elevated agriculture to the number three position.

Figure N-2: Nevada Operation

Nevada, lying as it does in the Great Basin, is part of the valley and range topography. North-south mountain ranges, elevated through faulting, separate numerous valleys. The geological sequence is slightly similar to South Africa's Rift Valley complex.

The most important river system in Nevada is the Humboldt River which forms from numerous tributaries at Deeth, 32 miles east of Elko, and flows westward close by Interstate 80. It ends at the Rye Patch Reservoir near Lovelock, a distance of 210 miles from origin. In the eastern part of the state, the White River rises out of the White Pine Mountains and flows south alongside highways 318 and 93 for a distance of 150 miles. Further south the mighty Colorado River with its impounded Lake Mead forms the border between Arizona and Nevada.

Of the 17 counties in the State of Nevada, placer gold of economic importance has been identified in 14 counties, at some 115 locations. Geologically the bulk of the showings are grouped in the northern and western part of the state. It is estimated that since the first placer was worked, in excess of 1.7 million ounces of gold have been recovered from placers within the state, while lode production, since the Comstock Lode discovery has accounted for an additional 24 million ounces. Not included in this estimate is a tremendous number of leach operations which came into existence in the last two decades, and provided large amounts of gold.

We will start our investigation of Nevada on the north run from Reno, in Washoe County.

Washoe County

Some 8 miles north of Reno on Highway 395, several roads lead west towards **Peavine Peak**. Gulches and ravines along the northeast slope have given rise to small placer deposits. Going south on 395 from Reno for 14 miles, some placer production came from the hills west of **Pleasant Valley** close by this road. A further 3 miles puts us at the junction of 395 and 27. Going east from this junction for nine miles on highway 27, brings us to the west flank of the Virginia Range in the **Jumbo District**. This was a late blooming placer district situated on the other side of the mountain range from the Comstock Lode. Going west from the 395-27 junction along highway 27 we travel up the east flank of the Carson Range to a point (roughly 6500 feet in elevation) where

Washoe Creek runs north-south in **Little Valley District**. This is part of a Tertiary structure, one often found in Nevada.

Figure N-3: Nevada Operation

Returning to Reno and going east on I-80 to Wadsworth at the junction with State highway 34. From here north for three miles then west for 6 miles to the **Olinghouse District** on the east flank of the Virginia Range. Olinghouse Canyon, Frank Free Canyon and Tiger Canyon plus tributary ravines have contributed over 2000 ounces of placer gold.

Continuing northeast along I-80, we pass through Churchill county, an unproductive placer area, into **Pershing County**, probably the #1 placer county in Nevada. Production has been estimated at greater than 730,000 ounces of gold from a total of 17 placer localities.

At Lovelock, 90 miles from Reno, a county dirt road leads north for 10 miles to **Trinity Canyon**, on the east flank of the

Trinity Range. Four old gold mines here have probably contributed some of their eroded gold to the gulches and canyons that etch back into this range. Check the gulches between here and Black Rock Canyon 3 1/2 miles further northeast. No road so you'll probably have to hoof it.

Almost due east of Lovelock, some 24 miles, is the **Rochester Mining District.** This area reached prominence when high grade silver veins were found on Menzil Hill in the Humboldt Range in 1911. Rochester canyon is best reached by state highway 50, east from Oreana on I-80. Some three miles back in the mountains, a series of old silver mines become prominent. Strangely enough, the occasional creeks and gulches run gold. This area is well staked; however try your panning exercises in this canyon, Limerick Canyon(one mile to the north) Sacramento Canyon and Gold Spring gulch. Highway 50 continues over the mountain range and down the east flank. Near the crest of the range, check out **Spring Valley Creek**. This is the location of the first dredge in Nevada in 1911. By going south along 50 at the road split, you can check out Dry Gulch, Troy Canyon, American Canyon, and South America Canyon. All have dirt roads accessing them. Going north on 50 for some seven miles a light duty road travel up **Buena Vista Creek** to Unionville (an abandoned village) and on to Congress Canyon, Wilson Canyon and Straight Canyon, all locations have had indications of gold.

Returning to I-80 at 9 1/2 miles north of Oreana, a road going west crosses the Rye Patch Dam and connects with a north-south unimproved road (Old Emigrant Road). Going north for 3 miles a dirt road goes west for the same distance to an alluvial fan area located close to **Majuba Hill** (Antelope District). Highgrade, close-to-surface placers were located here in 1938. This is a dry wash area if you can locate any open ground. Return to the Old Emigrant Road and continue on north (roughly 15 miles) until it intersects a similar road going west. Travel west for 12 miles then south for 7 miles to the **Placerites District** which is composed of ravines in the gravel hills just off the north end of the Seven Troughs Range. This again is dry wash with coarse gold in relatively shallow gravels.

Figure N-4: Loading Hopper

Back on I-80, at Imlay, 25 miles north of Oreana, the **Imlay Placer District** lies a few miles east of the highway in the western foothills of the Humboldt Range. Check the gravels in the canyons of Eldorado, Florida and Imlay. Mostly drywashing. The **Sierra District** is 8 miles east of Mill City, which is on I-80. Gravel roads lead to the northern end of the East Humboldt Range. Auriferous gravels have been found in Auburn, Barber, Wright, Rock Hill, Dun Glen, Spaulding

Canyons and at Willow Creek, 5 miles south along the east side of the range. Numerous shafts were sunk during the Depression years in the Dun Glen placers.

At Winnemucca, in **Humboldt County**, we travel up highway 95 for 13 miles then east on a gravel road across the Little Humboldt River and Paradise Valley to the west flank of the Hot Springs Range. The **Dutch Flat** placers are located in Sodarisi Canyon and El Paso Gulch. The deposits occur in stream gravels, fan alluvium and side hill benches. Lack of water in this area means dry washing.

Back on I-80 at Golconda (18 miles east of Winnemucca) we go south 10 miles on an unimproved road to the east flank of the Sonoma Range. Here in **Gold Run Creek** which empties into Ragan Creek, the upper portion of the creek has been sporadically placered since discovery in 1886.

Washoe County

Nearest Campground **Reno**

Bally's Camperland — 452 sites — open all year — deposit required — (702) 789-2000.

River's Edge RV Park — 164 sites — open all year — deposit required — (702) 358-8533

Motels **Reno** Numerous

Storey County

Nearest Campgrounds: *Virginia City*

Virginia City RV Park — 95 sites — open all year — deposit required — (702) 847-0999

Pershing County

Nearest Campgrounds: *Lovelock*

KOA — 70 sites — open all year — deposit required — (702) 273-2276

Rye Patch Recreation Area — 44 sites — open all year — state operated — (702) 558-7321

Motels: *Lovelock*

Sturgeon's Motel (Best Western) — 74 units — (702) 273-2971

Humboldt County

Nearest Campgrounds: Winnemucca Hi Desert RV — open all year — 152 sites — deposit required — (702) 623-4513

KOA — open all year — 150 sites — deposit required — (702) 623-5797

Motels: Winnemucca

Holiday Motel (Best Western) — 40 units — (702) -623-3684

Town House Motel — 19 units — (702) 623-3620

We now enter **Lander County** on I-80. There are 2 placer mining districts here; the first, **Battle Mountain** has a big history of placer production despite a late discovery in 1909. It had been known since 1866 for its lode production. The placer locations are 6 miles southwest of the village of Battle Mountain via highway 306.

The productive areas lie along the north, east and south slopes of the Battle Mountain Range. The various gulches on these slopes and the fans spreading from them into the valley have been highly productive. The southern flank includes Copper, Galena, Box, Philadelphia and Iron Canyons. The northern section includes Elder Canyon, Snow and Piute Gulches, while the east slope contains Copper Basin, Long, Licking Creek and Vail Canyons. In addition several creeks, primarily Rocky, Willow and Cottonwood have been productive in the past. The placers have seen dredge action with large mining interests being active. I doubt there is any open ground available but if you are in the area do check out the various placers from the historical standpoint. There is also a big open pit mine in this area and the potential for more open pits!

Figure N-5: Single Sluice

The **Hilltop** placer area is about 10 miles southeast of Battle Mountain village on the Mount Lewis road. Following up Rock Creek brings in Crum, Maysville and Hilltop Canyons, all of which have produced auriferous gravels.

Continuing on the Mount Lewis road for another 10 miles brings in the **Bullion** placers at Tenabo in the Shoshone Range. Immediately south of Tenabo, on the eastern flank of the Range, Mill, Triplett, Mud Springs, Rosebud and Tub Springs Gulches have seen prior placer production. Some of the production was by means of drift mining.

Continuing to travel east on I-80, we enter Eureka County. Only one placer deposit of consequence has been located here and that one is **Lynn Creek** in the northern part of the county. From Carlin on I-80, a road leads northwest to the Carlin Gold Mine, a distance of 18 miles. An additional 2 miles beyond brings in the placer creeks of Lynn, Simon, Sheep and Rodeo near the summit of the southern Tuscarora Range. The deposits were narrow but relatively rich, with variable thicknesses of overburden. They have been well worked over. This whole area is likely tightly staked due to the number of large open-pit gold mines in the area.

Travelling along I-80 we enter Elko County. Several rich placer areas have been exploited in the northern section of the county. These placer areas have in the last decade been developed into large open-pit gold mines. At Elko swing north up state highway 225 to **Mountain City**, a distance of 80 miles. Please note that this area north of Elko, hosts a huge number of large gold operations, both of the milling and leaching type. Because of this open ground might be at a premium.

Prior to Mountain City, at the Wild Horse Reservoir, a dirt road running northeast towards **Island Mountain** follows Penrod Creek upstream for 6 miles. The alluvial basin on the north side of Island Mountain has seen productive gravels in the past. Check the creeks percolating out of Hammond and Coleman Canyons and Hope Gulch. Just 6 miles south of Mountain City, the **Van Duzer** placers have yielded fair gold. Van Duzer and Cobb Creeks drain a hilly area east of the Owyhee River. Both creeks are permanent with gravel deposits up to 15 feet thick. Today the large Mountain City open pit occupies all this land and leaves little room for panning.

Although most of the ground around Mountain City is owned by mining companies, it might be fun and interesting to pan all streams entering the river. There is an Indian

Reservation just to the north of this area. It would be well to avoid operations in the reserve. At Owyhee village 12 miles north of Mountain City, State Highway 226 swings south and returns along the east side of the Bull Run Range. A number of large gold-silver mining operations are close to this highway.

At White Rock, 20 miles south of Owyhee, check the streams entering the river. Continue another 40 miles to a junction. Highway 226 continues southeast to join 225. However, travel west seven miles to **Tuscarora**. Placers here have had as high a production as Island Mountain. The low hills south and west of the city have yielded well in the past. Check Eureka, Review and Stovepipe Gulches and Gardner Ravine. However the large open-pit heap leach operation here might make access difficult if not impossible. Continue to Elko.

Elko County

Nearest Campground: Elko (125 miles from *Winnemucca*)

KOA — 117 sites — open all year — deposit required — (702) 738-689

Mountain City —32 sites — open May 23 to Oct. 15 — National Forests — (702) 763-6691

Motels: *Battle Mountain*

Big Chief Motel (Best Western) — 58 units — (702) 635-2416

Elko

Gold Rush Inn (Best Western) — 109 units — (702) 738-8787

Rodeway Inn — 65 units — restaurant — (702) 738-7000

Having completed the northern leg of our placer expedition we now start back west from Elko. We head south along route 228 towards Jiggs (33 miles). Continue on this route for

24 miles then swing onto 892 just prior to Railroad Pass. Stay on this dirt road for 18 miles to the north end of Newark Valley. Dirt roads run 8 miles east from here to the south slope of **Big Bald Mountain**, in the Ruby Range at an elevation of 7,400 feet. These placers yielded nuggets of 0.07 to 0.29 grade ($25 to $100). The principle location was Water Canyon and its tributary ravines. Return south on 892 for 35 miles to I-50 and east for 59 miles to Ely. Continue east on I-50 to **Osceola**, a distance of 38 miles. This is an old and famous placer district (1877) located on the west flank of the Snake Range. The gravels are of the dry variety and vary in thickness from 10 to over 200 feet. Hydraulic and shaft sinking was performed on some of the placers. The better gold areas of the past were Dry Gulch, Mary Ann Canyon (alluvial fan), Grub Gulch on the west side and Weaver Creek and the Summit workings on the east slope.

Returning to Ely we travel westward on I-50 to Eureka (77 miles). The hills just north of the town produced minor amounts of gold from bench gravels. Carry westward to Austin, 70 miles further. The Reese River which passes close by Austin has had auriferous gravels mined on occasions. Return east for 12 miles to highway 376, a very scenic route heading south from I-50.Four miles south of the intersection **Birch Creek**, an intermittent creek, cuts across the highway. Shafts were sunk here to check the gold streaks at bedrock. Check out any active streams cutting across the roadway while heading south, in particular Ophir and Clear Creeks, and Jett and Pablo, further south. Fifty-five miles south of the intersection, near **Round Mountain**, we enter a well known placer area. The south, east and west sides of Round Mountain and the Toquima Range have yielded close to 250,000 ounces of gold since discovery in 1906. Gold is found throughout the gravels which are thinnest against the mountain, thickening as they enter the valley. If you can do any panning here, fine, but I doubt you will find any open ground. Check out Willow, Moore and Jefferson Creeks north of Round Mountain if possible. A further 11 miles to the south is the famous **Manhattan District**. It is 7 miles east of 376 on route 377 at the south end of the Toquima Range. This area has been worked by shafts and drifts, sluices, drywashers and a bucket-line dredge. The area was discovered the same year as Round Mountain (1906) and has produced better than 225,000 ounces of gold. A unique development at Manhattan was the discovery of gold in four different gravel locations —

(1) very high level patches representing the origin deposits

(2) bench gravels on canyon walls from the later downcutting action

(3) the gulch channel gravels, and

(4) recent erosional debris found on hillside washes.

The placer areas are Manhattan Gulch as the main location with Giffin Gulch and Slaughterhouse Gulch as other prominent locations. Manhattan Gulch has been drift-mined over a 5 mile length; it has an average width of 300 feet; the gravel deposits vary from 20 to 100 feet with a bedrock pay streak being two to 4 feet thick. A good number of the operations are of the lessee type.

Out of Manhattan take the improved road across 376 which leads to another dirt road which slides around the south end of the Toiyabe Mountains and heads north along the west side of these mountains, over the Shoshone Mountains to **Ione**, a distance of 73 miles. We are still in Nye County. Several small placers, northwest and southwest of the town have shallow gravels and are amenable to drywashing. Across the Ione Valley on the east slope of the **Paradise Range** are small placers close to lode deposits. Continue north on the Eastgate-Ione road to I-50 (39 miles).Along I-50 to 6 miles west of Frenchman to the **Sand Springs** placer located in the Sand Springs Range, a quarter of a mile south of the interstate in Churchill County. Return to Frenchman and take State Highway 31 south for a distance of 29 miles, just north of Alkali Flat. The washes and canyons of the hills (Black Eagle Hills) to the north have alluvial fans which carry minor amounts of placer gold. This is known as the **Eagleville District**. A few miles to the west is the **Rawhide** placers which were located in 1907 and which has produced in the vicinity of 10,000 ounces. Continue south for 56 miles to Hawthorne. Follow I-95 north to Yerington (58 miles). There are two close by placers in this built-up area.

Figure N-6: Nevada Operation

The **Yerington** placers are reached by a road going west from a point 10 miles north of Yerington towards the Singatse Ranges. Two miles south of Gallagher Pass an unimproved road leads to the placers. Remnants of an old Tertiary channel are found in a stream channel cutting across this range. The gravels are some 20 feet thick. Continuation of this Tertiary channel was noted some 2 miles to the southwest in the low hills between Lincoln Flat and Smith Valley. These placers are called the **Buckskin** placers. Several placers are grouped around Wishart Hill. Past operations of these placers have been conducted by lode mining companies of the area.

Nearest Campgrounds: Ely

Cave Lake — 36 sites — open all year —State operated — (702) 728-4467

KOA — 110 sites —open all year — private — (702) 289-3413

Tonopah

Pine Creek — 22 sites — May to mid Oct. — National Forests — (702) 482-6286

Fallon

Fallon RV Park — 45 sites — open all year — (702) 867-2332

Lahontan Recreation Area — 53 sites — open all year — State operated — (702) 867-3500

Hawthorne

Walker Lake — 17 sites — open all year — BLM operated — (702) 882-1631

We have completed our central swing of the placer areas and will now go to the southern section starting at Yerington and continuing down I-95 to Hawthorne and on to Mina, travelling a distance of 90 miles.

At Mina, some placer gold has been recovered from the **Excelsior Mountain** washes several miles south of the highway. Dirt roads lead south towards these mountains. All washes and canyons should be checked. Unfortunately they are dry washes. Some 23 miles south of Mina on highway 360 is **Candelaria**, a large open-pit silver mine. The Monte Cristo Range, in the vicinity, has placered gold in the past along its north and west slopes.

Figure N-7: Nevada Hopper in Action

Further along I-95 at the great mining camp of **Tonopah**, the San Antonio Mountains have shown auriferous washes in the past. Further south at Goldfields, 22 miles south of Tonopah, placer has been reported from **Klondyke** area. It is not a strong placer area.

Forty-nine miles south of Tonopah highway 266 heads west from I-95. Continue southwest for 15 miles to **Gold Point**. Late discovery (1946) placers are credited with minor production from the canyons of Slate Ridge and Mount Ogden.

At the split of 266, follow west to **Lida**, where 5 miles west, an unimproved road branches south to Tule Canyon, located between Magruder Mountain (close to Lida) and Sylvania Mountain, off to the west. More than 5000 ounces were placered from here. Placers, discovered in 1876, are located near the head of the canyon and were worked for some 4-6 miles down the canyon, plus its tributaries.

Four miles further along 266, a dirt road leads south to the **Palmetto Wash** placers, located at the northwest end of the Sylvania Mountains. These placers are intermittent in operation and small scale. May not be too unlikely an area to investigate for your own placer location.

Return to I-95 and continue south to Beatty. Weak placers have been reported from the intermittent **Amargosa River** and from the washes on the west slope of **Bare Mountain**, and the **Bullfrog Hills**. The placers are of the dry-wash type and some of the gravels have proven deep.

Highway 160 splits off from I-95, some 45 miles south of Beatty. **Johnnie** is 10 miles down the line with placers being reported in the low hills of the Spring Mountains north and south of the town. Gulch and hillside gravels have contributed to the reported 500 ounces of placer gold attributed to this area. The rich pay streaks are often at the base of 25 foot thick gravel beds. Several lode gold mines have been located in the Johnnie area.

Continuing on I-95 to Las Vegas, picking up I-15 and travelling northeast to Glendale, is a distance of 122 miles. Here, in Clarke County, placer gold was extracted from bottom land gravels of the **Muddy River** at several points. One of the placer areas was 4 miles downstream from its junction with Meadow Valley Wash while the other location is outside Logandale, 7 miles below Glendale. The gold is very fine and the gravels are thick.

Continue northeast on I-15 to Riverside where route 170 crosses the Virgin River and continues south for 37 miles to the **Gold Butte** area. Placers here are 2 to 20 feet thick with very fine gold generally lying on bedrock and associated with large amounts of black sand. The placers are in an area between Mud Wash and Virgin Mountains.

Nearest Campgrounds: Hawthorne

Walker Lake — 17 sites — open all year — BLM operated — (702) 882-1631

Beatty (Death Valley in California)

7 locations totalling over 1500 sites operated by National Park Service — (619) 786-2331

Las Vegas

Circusland RV Park — 421 sites — open all year — deposit required — private — (702) 794-3757

4 sites run by National Forest — (702) 388-625

Overton

Valley of Fire — 49 sites — open all year — State park — (702) 397-2088.

Motels: *Hawthorne*

El Capitan — restaurant — (702) 945-3321

Tonopah

Hi Desert Inn (Best Western) — (702) 482-3511

Jim Butler Inn — (702) 482-3577

Las Vegas

Numerous

Beatty

Burro Inn — 63 units — (702) 553-2225

We have now complete our placer tour of the southwestern states. We are ready to move into the northwest — Idaho, Montana, Wyoming and Utah in search of more placer areas so that we can continue to GO FOR THE GOLD.

BIBLIOGRAPHIES

Gold Bearing Gravels of the Ancestral Yuba River, Sierra Nevada, CA......G. S. Prof. Paper 772...(1974) ... Warren E. Yeend.

Geology of Northern California...Cal.Division of Mines& Geology...Bulletin 190...(1976)...Various Authors.

Gold in Placer Deposits ...U.S. Geological Survey Bulletin 1857G...(1989)...Warren E. Yeend.

Outlines of Geology...Wiley & Sons ...(1941)...Longwell et Al.

Placer Mining in Nevada...Nev.Bureau of Mines & Geology...Bulletin 27...(1936)...W.O.Vandenburg.

Gold Resources in the Tertiary Gravels of California...Bureau of Interior...(1968)...Roland W. Merwin.

Arizona Lode Gold Mines & Gold Mining...Arizona Bureau of Geology & Mineral Technology...Bulletin 137 (1934)...Wilson,Cunningham & Butler.

Placer Gold Recovery Methods...Cal.Dept. of Conservation...Special Publication 87...Michael Silva.

Placer Gold Deposits of Nevada...Geol. Survey Bulletin 1356...(1973)...Maureen G. Johnson.

Placer Gold Deposits of Arizona...G.S.Bulletin 1355... (1981)...Maureen G. Johnson.

Gold Districts of California...Cal. Division of Mines & Geology Bulletin 193...(1963)...W.B. Clarke.

Geology of Placer Deposits...Cal.Division of Mines & Geology Special Publication 34...(1964)...A.P. Jenkins.

Handbook of Mineral Dressing...Wiley Handbook Series ...(1927)...A.F.Taggart.

Gold Placers &Placering in Arizona...Arizona Geological Survey Bulletin 168...(1961)

Fine Sluice Recovery of Selected Sluicebox Configuration ...U.B.C. Program 3...(1989)...G.W.Poling.

Basic Placer Mining...Cal.Division of Mines & Geology Special Publication 41...(1963).

Dear Purchaser:

This is the first book of a planned series of four. The next book will venture into the Northwestern States — Idaho, Montana, Wyoming and Utah. There will be updating of the early chapters with new innovations and additions. With respect to the States themselves, the same format will apply — that is placer areas, possibilities, campgrounds and local motels. To give us an idea of how this series is being received and whether you would like a copy of Book Two we would appreciate receiving the attached letter. We will acknowledge your letter and advise you of the production date of the next book.Thank You.

Price Publishing,
P.O. Box 8195-186,
Blaine,WA 98230.

Please inform me when the next book "GO FOR THE GOLD' — (Idaho, Montana, Wyoming and Utah) will be ready for distribution.

Name ______________________________

Address ____________________________

City & Zip Code _______________________

Comments ___________________________

____